NEXT GENERATION TOURISM—TOUCHING THE GROUND LIGHTLY

NEXT GENERATION TOURISM— TOUCHING THE GROUND LIGHTLY

YALE SCHOOL OF ARCHITECTURE
THE EDWARD P. BASS VISITING DISTINGUISHED ARCHITECTURE FELLOWSHIP

JOHN SPENCE
HENRY SQUIRE
PATRICK BELLEW
TIMOTHY NEWTON

EDITED BY NINA RAPPAPORT AND RUKSHAN VATHUPOLA

Published by:
Yale School of Architecture
180 York Street
New Haven, Connecticut 06511
www.architecture.yale.edu

Distributed by:
Actar
440 Park Ave. South
New York, NY 10016
www.actar.com

This publication was made possible through the Edward P. Bass Distinguished Visiting Architecture Fellowship fund of the Yale School of Architecture. Published through the dean's office, it is the fourteenth publication in the Bass Fellowship's series.

Dean: Deborah Berke
Associate Dean: Philip Bernstein

Publications Director: Nina Rappaport
Assistant Editor: Rukshan Eranga Vathupola
Copy Editor: Cathryn Drake
Design: MGMT. design

ISBN: 978-1-94876530

THE EDWARD P. BASS DISTINGUISHED VISITING ARCHITECTURE FELLOWSHIP

In 2003 Edward P. Bass, a 1967 graduate of Yale College who studied at the Yale School of Architecture as a member of the class of 1972, endowed this fellowship to bring property developers to the school to lead advanced studios in collaboration with design faculty. An environmentalist and developer, Bass sponsored the Biosphere 2 development in Oracle, Arizona, in 1991, and is responsible for the ongoing revitalization of downtown Fort Worth, Texas, where his Sundance Square, which combines restoration with new construction, has transformed a moribund urban core into a vibrant regional center. In all of his work Bass has been guided by the conviction that architecture is a socially engaged art operating at the intersection of grand visions and everyday realities.

The Bass Fellowship ensures that the school curriculum recognizes the role of the property developer as an integral part of the design process. The program brings developers to Yale to work alongside educators and architecture students in the studio and situate the discussion about architecture in the wider discourse of contemporary practice. The first Bass Studio, led by Gerald Hines and Louis I. Kahn Visiting Professor Stefan Behnisch in 2005, was documented in *Poetry, Property, and Place* (2006). The following year Stuart Lipton, Saarinen Visiting Professor Sir Richard

Rogers ('62), engineer Chris Wise, and architect Malcolm Smith (MArch '97) teamed up for the second Bass Studio, documented in *Future-Proofing* (2007). *The Human City: Kings Cross* (2008) records the Yale studio collaboration between Roger Madelin and Bishop Visiting Professor Demetri Porphyrios. *Urban Integration: Bishopsgate Goods Yard* (2009) documents the studio led by Nick Johnson and the FAT architecture partnership; in 2010 architect David M. Schwarz (MArch '74) and Charles Atwood's studio project was published in *Learning in Las Vegas*. The book *Urban Intersections: São Paulo* (2011) documents the studio led by real estate developer Katherine Farley and architect Deborah Berke. Hong Kong developer Vincent Lo joined Saarinen Visiting Professors Paul Katz, Jamie von Klemperer, and Forth Bagley (BA '99, MArch '01) for the studio described in the book *Rethinking Chongquing: Mixed Use and Super Dense* (2014). Next *Social Infrastructure: New York* (2015) features the studio led by real estate developer Douglas Durst and Bjarke Ingles, of BIG. Furthering the series, Dutch developer Isaäc Kalisvaart and Yale's Alexander Garvin (BA '62, MArch '67), Andrei Harwell, and Kevin Gray describe their studio in *The Marine Etablissement* (2016). *A Sustainable Bodega and Hotel* (2017) brought together resort property developer John Spence, of the Karma Royal Group, and Saarinen Visiting professors Patrick Bellew, of Atelier Ten, and Andy Bow, of Foster + Partners. *Paranoazinho: City-Making Beyond Brasilia* (2017) presents the analysis and studio led by real estate developers Rafael Birmann and Ricardo Birmann, of São Paulo, and associate professor (adjunct) Sunil Bald. The studio research and projects led by real estate developer Jonathan Rose with Louis I. Kahn Visiting Assistant Professors Sara Caples (MArch '74) and

and Everardo Jefferson (MArch '75) were the subject of *Harlem: Mart 125* (2018). The Michael Samuelian and Simon Hartmann Bass studio with Andrei Harwell (MArch '06) was featured in the exhibition on display on Governors Island in New York and its accompanying publication *...And More* in May 2019. And the book *Diamonds of American Cities,* by Janet Marie Smith, senior vice president for planning and development for the Los Angeles Dodgers, with Yale faculty Alan Plattus and Andrei Harwell, was published in 2020. With this new publication format we feature John Spence who returned to Yale a second time with sustainability expert Patrick Bellew, London architect Henry Squire, and Tim Newton (MArch '06) to lead us on new visions for eco-resorts.

STUDIO INTRO-DUCTION

It is said that our actions impact the environment seven generations into the future. In fact the growing concern about the global impact of tourism and the associated waste produced by leisure industries is outdated. This Yale graduate advanced architecture studio analyzed the current ecological conditions, indigenous architecture styles, and resort culture of Gili Meno, a tiny remote island off the coast of Lombok, Indonesia, to generate next-generation models of tourism. John Spence, head of the Karma Group, which owns properties in Bali and Gili Meno; Henry Squire, of Squire and Partners architects, in London; Patrick Bellew, principal of London-based sustainability firm Atelier Ten; and critic in architecture Timothy Newton ('06) asked students to create projects aligned with the studio brief for a specific resort clientele and program. The students' ambitions for insightful sustainable projects to inspire future resorts focused on local and ethical resources, recycling, and environmental responsibility.

The students' investigations into the long-term ecological and resort history of Gili Meno informed their proposals for environmental and holistic resort designs. During the studio trip to Bali they visited several resorts and met with material experts, local architects, and designers. While staying at two Karma resorts on Bali and Gili Meno, the students experienced the inner workings of the island resorts firsthand as well as the transportation networks between the two islands. They learned about the distinctions between spaces for staff and visitors and the need to interweave two distinct programs for front and back of house. The students met with renowned Canadian bamboo designer Elora Hardy, founder of design studio IBUKU, at the international Green School in Bali, which she designed. There they learned about new innovations in using miniature wooden models and parabolic designs for bamboo and local Indonesian architecture. The students also met with local construction workers to see bamboo being cut, dried, prepared, and shipped for construction. These experiences informed their designs for innovative projects based on established models of commercial tourism and ecological design.

Architectural sustainability expert Patrick Bellew worked with the students on the design of innovative ecological systems such as seaweed farming for ocean conservation, electric bio rocks for coral reef restoration, and solar farms to generate off-grid electricity to address issues of climate change. By integrating local materials such as volcanic rock, bamboo, and timber, the students created sustainable solutions that reduce material waste in the supply chain. With John Spence they explored the fiscal realities of hotel construction, generating projected revenue models by calculating guest rates and developing the intricate spatial relationships between guests and staff at a tropical resort. Architects Henry Squire and Timothy Newton provided insight on each student's project development through relevant architectural precedents, academic references, and examples of exceptional drawings, along with weekly critical feedback.

The students' concepts resulted in three distinct project types. New Models of Tourism proposes a new resort clientele with a new program offering once-in-a-lifetime experiences on the island. One proposal focused on nurturing romantic relationships by transforming the island into a getaway where the guests could arrive individually at a beach bar and couple up, then move inland for dinner at a restaurant garden. Ecological Architecture integrates a greater degree of sustainable systems, materials, and construction into resorts. A student proposed a bamboo resort floating above the coral reef that generated electricity from the motion of the waves, leaving the main site a farm to grow crops and graze livestock to supply the island. Health Resorts focuses on restoring the mental and physical health of guests, who would come to Gili Meno to escape the fast-paced industrialized world. One proposal employed Indonesian rituals of pottery and weaving in health and wellness centers where guests calm body and mind while learning about local culture through the art forms.

The book opens with an interview between architect Henry Squire and Nina Rappaport concerning the design and evolution of Squire and Partners' projects. The second section analyzes students' research into commercial and environmental precedents. The studio brief outlines the ecological, architectural, and programmatic parameters provided to the students, followed by presentations of individual student projects categorized into the three distinct types: New Models of Tourism, Ecological Architecture, and Health Resorts. Finally, John Spence discusses the present incorporation of ecological design elements into the Karma resorts, including the corporate response to the COVID-19 crisis.

The editors would like to recognize the valuable contributions of the students in the classes of 2020 and 2021 to the production of this book under the challenging constraints presented by COVID-19: Justin Tsang, Smit Patel, Anna Borou Yu, Baolin Paul Shen, Rukshan Eranga Vathupola, Laélia Kim-Lan Vaulot, I-Ting Tsai, Cristina Anastase, Samantha Monge Kaser, Jenna Ritz, and Elaine Cui.

—Nina Rappaport and Rukshan Eranga Vathupola

Brick detail of Kingwood residential development, London SW1, 2017

INTERVIEW WITH HENRY SQUIRE

This interview was originally published in the Fall 2019 issue of Constructs.

NINA RAPPAPORT: How did you get connected to teaching Yale?

HENRY SQUIRE: It was through Patrick Bellew. He and I worked together on a few key projects that all have a sustainability focus including the new Chelsea Barracks in London, which is the only LEED-ND Platinum master plan outside the U.S. and on a major urban regeneration project in Doha where all the buildings also achieved LEED Platinum. This shared interest in sustainable architecture contributed to wonderful collaborations and then to teaching!

Your booming practice started out as your father's firm. How did it evolve into Squire & Partners over the past twenty-five years?

Obviously I've been working there since I was a knee-high photocopier. When I joined the practice in 1997, after graduating from the Royal College of Art, there were twenty people in the South Kensington office, and it slowly grew over the years. Working with family is always a difficult thing to do—and it's definitely tested our relationship at times—but after having come out on the other side, we would both say it was a very good experience. My father was a stabilizing force when I was young and full of enthusiasm. He would say, "Okay, that's great, but it doesn't work." It was a good mix of exuberant people with slightly more experience, which meant that we clashed at times. But that is also the reason the practice is what it is today.

How did your father expand the partnership?

Agriculture Technology Centre, Krong Samraong, Cambodia, 2018

Dad got wiped out in the big property crash of 1989, and his practice went from sixty to six people almost overnight. The analogy is the practice of burning crops from the year before to allow new grass to grow. In some ways that's why Tim Gledstone, Murray Levinson, and I are in the practice, and we are now trying to make that renewal happen again for the next generation.

You could compare it to the renewal of architecture with each generation. What is your approach to historical context as a way of creating with new materials and scales? Do you have a standard method, or do you approach each project differently?

There are architects who are on a crusade for a particular style and design the same type of building irrespective of location, but we treat each site specifically. We have done a lot at very sensitive locations in central London, and our work is considered to be quite sympathetic to the context and yet contemporary. If we were doing a building

in Shanghai, we might design something quite outrageous because that's the context there. We feel that London is a tapestry with broken bits, and we are weaving something of its time into it. You must learn from history and make a building feel familiar because that's how the city works, but you must also make sure that it is seen to be contemporary. We don't do pastiche. I will never design a building with a Corinthian column, but I'm not afraid of doing a building with a contemporary column. If we need to be sensitive, we can draw on DNA from the past but give it a contemporary twist. Sometimes we look to the history of the site to see where we can be a bit more expressive. It tells more stories than just the architectural ideas we're imposing.

You often experiment with new materials or craft old materials in a new way, such as the terra-cotta and metal leaf in the Mayfair project. How has that approach evolved from your more standard brick projects? How have you reinterpreted traditional materials for today?

We have been using CNC and computer technology to carve bricks and have developed a way recreate old crafts using modern technology. This allows our designers to tell stories in buildings and use ornamentation for its own sake. It is a return to an age of decoration; it is part of the architectural process that modern technologies are helping in new ways.

In the intriguing acrylic facade of the Reiss Headquarters, you employed a contemporary material using a different process. How is that related to the specificity of the site?

This is different because retailer David Reiss bought a building just behind Oxford Street and wanted to attract people's attention as they walk by and look down the side street. We wanted something dramatic and eye-catching, so we designed the facade as a veil that could change colors with the fashion seasons. It was a very specific response to the location, the brief, and the user—a fashion house.

How do you collaborate on projects with so many artisans and designers from different fields? Do you work in tandem or independently, with them as consultants?

We see ourselves as composers of a piece of music that we don't play. So we have an orchestra comprised of people who are better than we are at making, building, and crafting the details. Collaboration is key to everything we do. We have a slightly out-of-focus overall vision, and these skilled craftspeople and artisans help bring it into focus by doing things that we couldn't do. You get more out of the process if you're open-minded, and your collaborators become invested in it because they have ownership of the project as well.

What project would you say taught you a different way of looking at something through your collaborators—perhaps your own multifunctional office, in the former Brixton Department Store?

The office project was achieved by being on-site every single day and, as the workers exposed another layer of paint, saying, "Yes, that's nice." And when they'd chip away a bit of plaster, "Well, that's good too." It was a real voyage of discovery and very collaborative in a creative way. It had been painted a cream color, and we were stripping

View from Ferndale Road of the Department Store, London SW9, 2017

MUSIC
THE DEPARTMENT STORE
Nationwide

back layers of paint and plaster to reveal the building's history. We developed all the metalwork with a metalsmith; the furniture was coordinated with all the creative people in a voyage of discovery.

The Department Store was also a project you invested in. How did you decide to buy your own office building?

Our firm was scattered in satellite offices around King's Cross and we didn't want to be so dispersed. Our lease was up, and the rent renewal was just crazy—a 200 percent increase—so we couldn't afford to stay. We were looking for places to rent and fell in love with this building. We realized that owning the building would protect us from being priced out of our offices. Not only does it allow us to control our own destiny, but it is such an amazing building that it gave us the chance to show the world what we can do more quickly than in the average architecture project.

Squire & Partners works at a variety of scales, from small buildings like the agriculture center in Cambodia to major master-planning projects. What would you say links all of these programs?

The link is in terms of an attitude toward context and place. While we all love doing small, beautifully crafted projects, they happen once in a lifetime. I've been working on Chelsea Barracks for ten years, and at times it became wrapped up in politics and other things way beyond our control. The small projects are where you can express yourself. It's also great for the younger people in the office: they get a chance to really run a project rather than a door schedule for two and a half years. Building a little project in Cambodia is exciting for them. If you work at only one scale you lose your skills in terms of the other scales. It's important that the whole firm not get bogged down in very big projects.

How did you initiate the community and school projects in Africa and Cambodia?

Many of them came from younger staff members who were interested in these sorts of projects that they wanted to continue, and we've always supported people in our firm who come forward and say, "I'd like to do some charity work."

You're also an entrepreneur and own a golf-simulation center in London. How did you get into that?

It's a bit mad. Dad has always been an entrepreneur, and it has helped support the firm throughout the dark times. I fell in love with golf, so I went into this business, Urban Golf, with about twenty mates all investing a little bit. I think it's good for an architect to understand lots of different facets of the world that they can bring back into architecture in some way, shape, or form.

What new project do you find most exciting right now?

I've just won a pitch for two projects. We have been asked to make a five-mile, eight-lane stretch of road in Abu Dhabi more walkable, livable, and environmentally friendly for the public. We went there and had this crazy idea to make it into sections, like the bridges of London about which kids say, "Let's go and see that intersection because they have an amazing bridge, water feature, and light installation." We are working with environmental engineers to make the atmospheric conditions suitable for the climate. It will be sculpture meets installation meets urban regeneration as a catalyst for bringing people to the center. Another project is in a bad bit of suburban London, just outside the M25, where the question has been, "What is the city center of the future?" Retail, downtowns, and transport are changing massively. We have approached the project by looking to the past since some of the most loved city centers are those with narrow streets. We are considering how modern technologies, transport networks, and waste systems interface with an ancient typology.

ABOVE: The Department Store Interior, London SW9, 2017

OPPOSITE: Chelsea Barracks Phase 1, London SW1, 2019

STUDIO RESEARCH

In the weeks leading up to the Bali trip the students divided into teams of two or three. They researched the climate; the local building materials; the established infrastructure on Gili Meno, Indonesia, in relation to procuring clean drinking water, electricity, recycling, and excess rainwater; examples of resorts demonstrating the use and cost of air-conditioning in tropical climates; the necessary number of available rooms; and energy expenditure per year. The students compiled and presented this information during their visit to the Karma resorts in Bali.

GILI MENO CLIMATE DATA

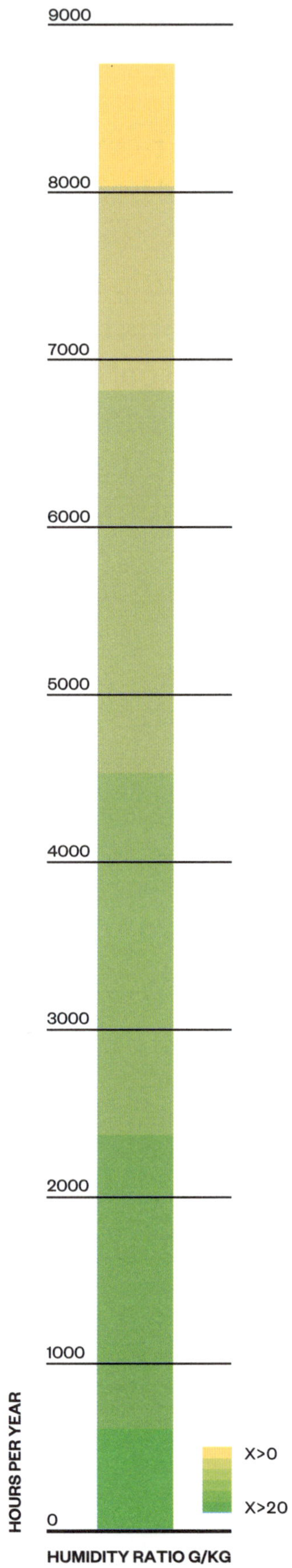

The Gili Islands lie within the warm tropical climate belt along the equator, in the southern hemisphere. The local microclimate is defined by an annual oscillation between the dry season and the rainy monsoon season. Because the Gili Islands are situated between two large active volcanoes, Mount Agung to the east and Mount Rinjani to the west, the precipitation is drawn away to the wetter tropical rain-forest climates on the adjacent islands of Bali and Lombok. However the months from November to March are dominated by tropical monsoons, causing annual precipitation to be as high as 67 inches per year. There is little variation in temperature, with lows remaining around 70° F and highs getting slightly over 90° F. The prevailing wind directions favor the southeast, at less than 5 m/s. Due to their proximity to the equator, the Gili Islands get approximately 12 hours of daylight each day throughout the year. Located within the Ring of Fire, the islands are prone to earthquakes and minor tremors as a result of ongoing plate tectonics, along with volcanic activity. The warm waters that surround the islands are relatively shallow and home to various coral reefs and deepwater dive sites.

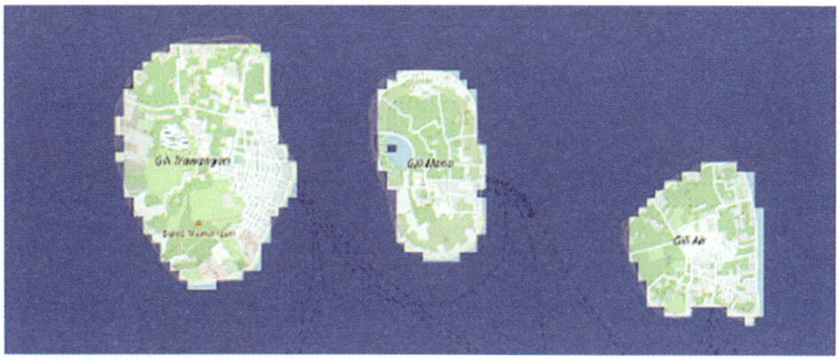

CURRENT SEA LEVEL

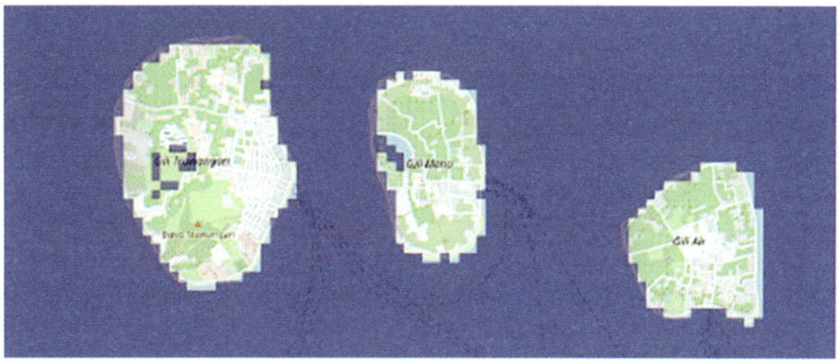

+ 3M

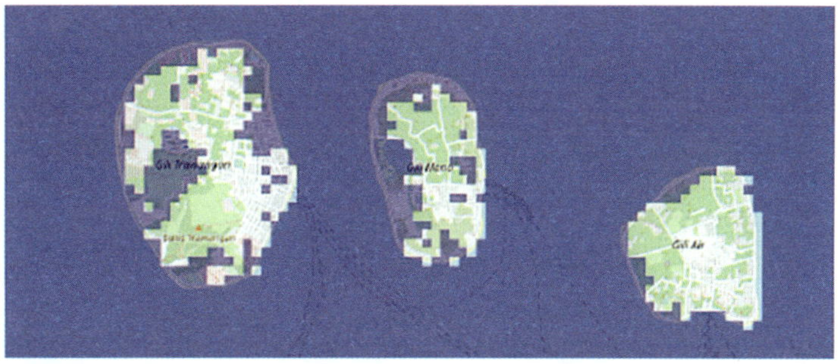

+6M

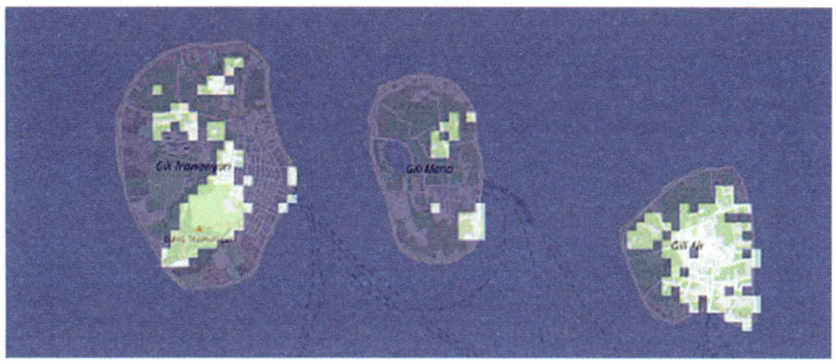

+9M

RIGHT: Map of sea-level rise on the islands with a difference of 3, 6, and 9 meters

OPPOSITE: Humidity ratio frequency

Overlooking the site on the island of Gili Meno

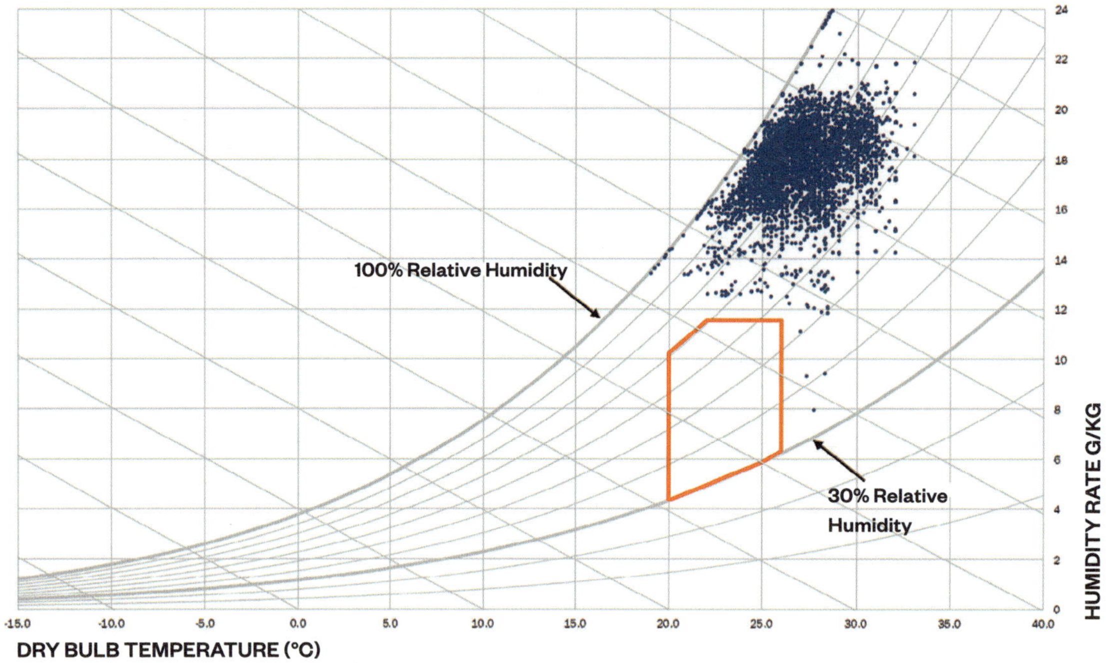

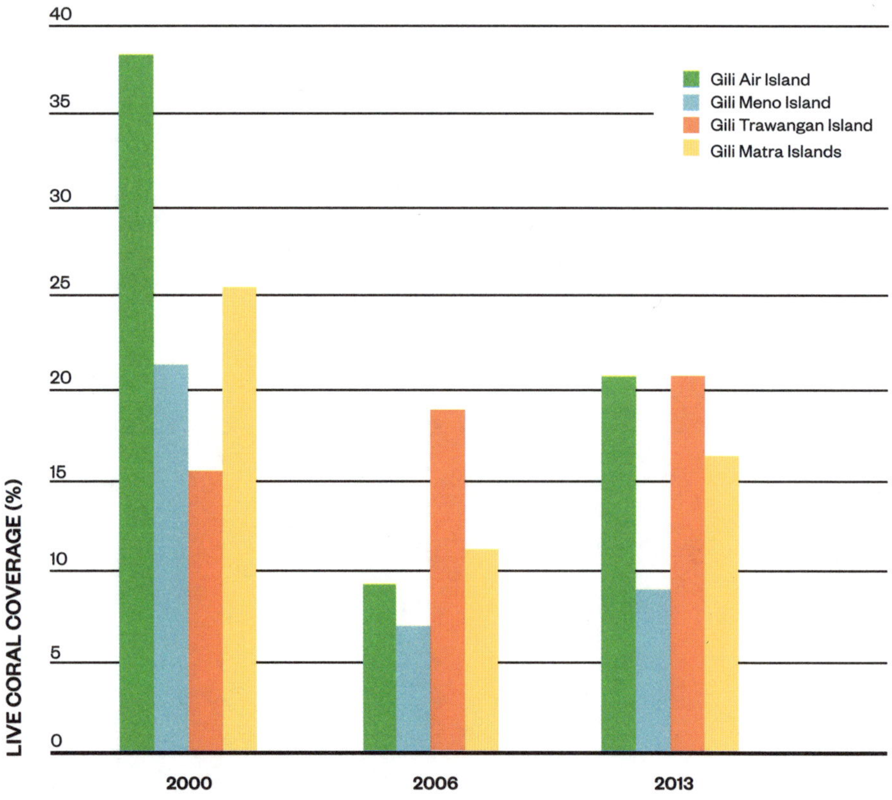

TOP: Psychrometric chart for Gili Islands

BOTTOM: Chart of live coral coverage changes in Gili Matra region 2000/2006/2013

OPPOSITE TOP: Annual wind direction and frequency

OPPOSITE BOTTOM: Gili Meno sun path

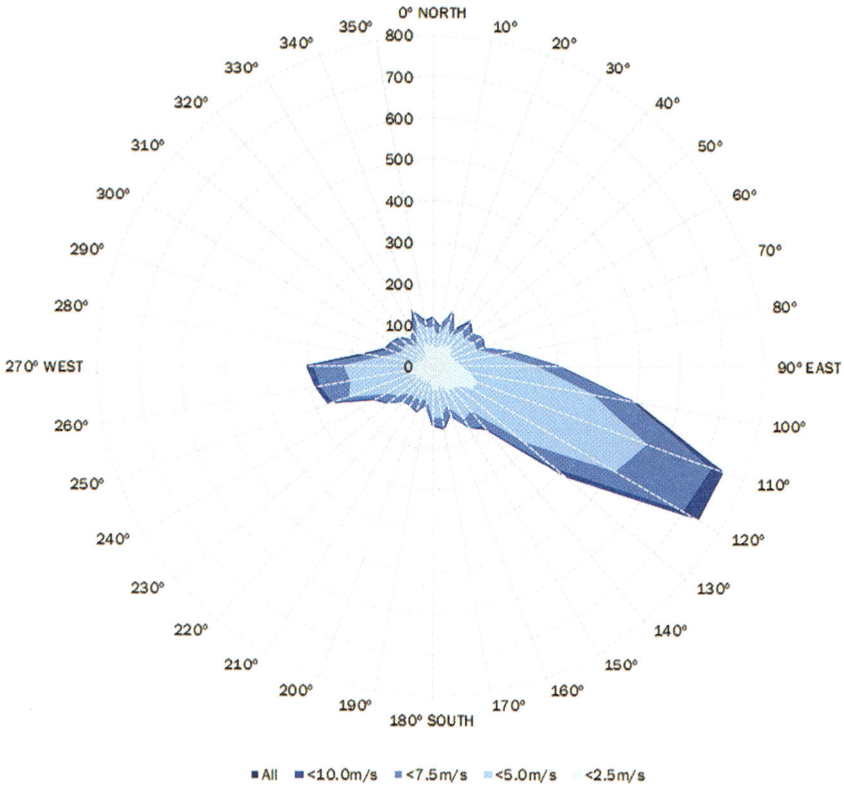
0° NORTH
10°
20°
30°
40°
50°
60°
70°
80°
90° EAST
100°
110°
120°
130°
140°
150°
160°
170°
180° SOUTH
190°
200°
210°
220°
230°
240°
250°
260°
270° WEST
280°
290°
300°
310°
320°
330°
340°
350°
800
700
600
500
400
300
200
100
0
All
<10.0m/s
<7.5m/s
<5.0m/s
<2.5m/s

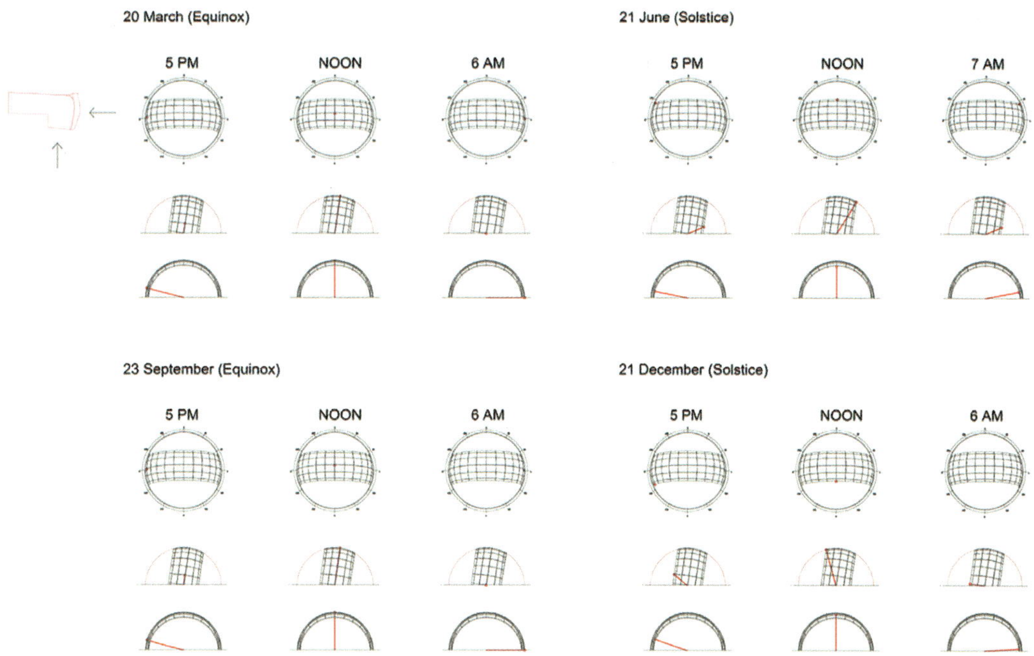
20 March (Equinox)
5 PM
NOON
6 AM
21 June (Solstice)
5 PM
NOON
7 AM
23 September (Equinox)
5 PM
NOON
6 AM
21 December (Solstice)
5 PM
NOON
6 AM

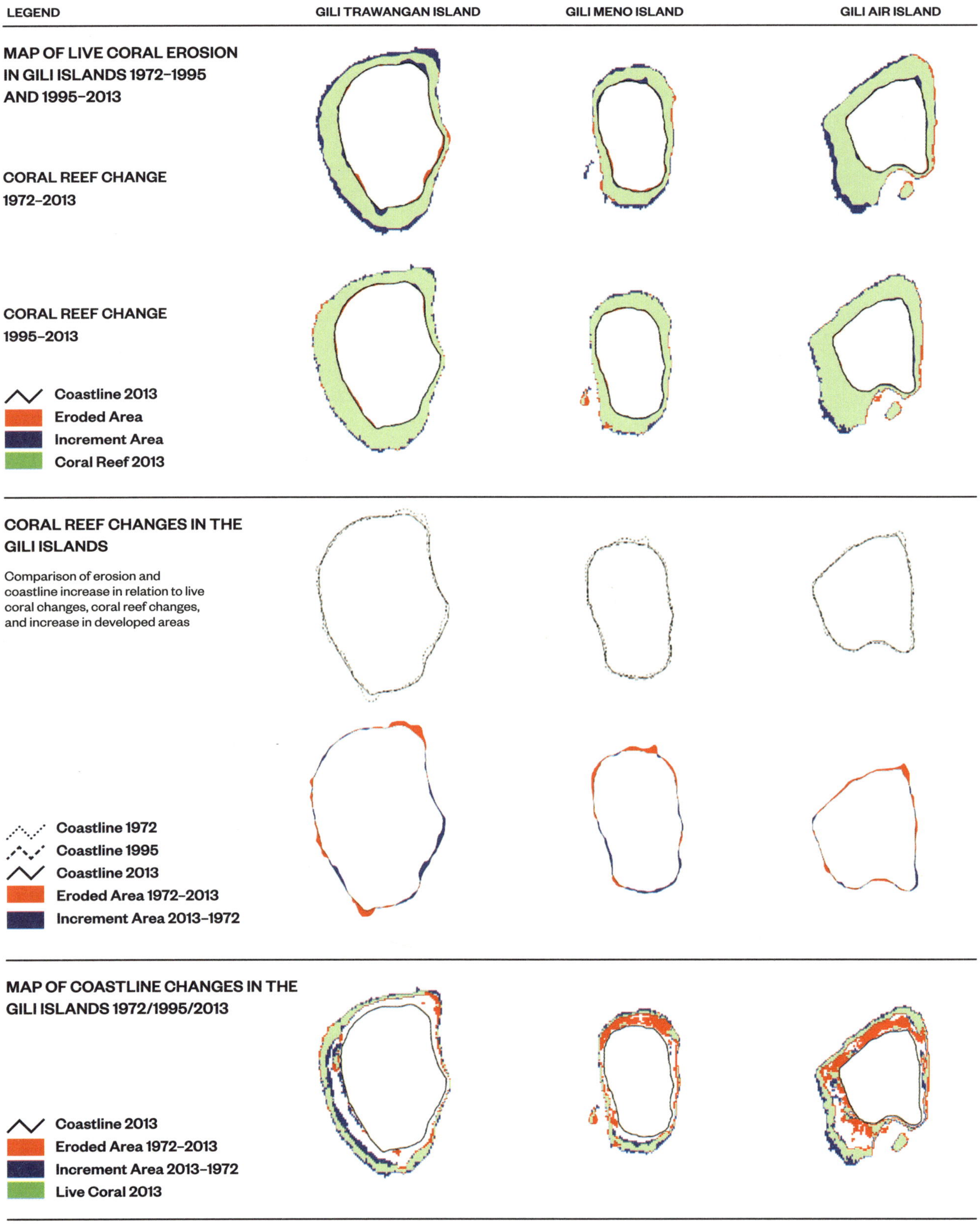

N
500 1,000 2,000 Meters

Map of sea-level rise on the islands with a difference of 3, 6, and 9 meters

LOCAL INFRASTRUCTURE

Water Infrastructure and transport in Gili Meno

The lack of fresh water is one of the more severe resource issues on Gili Meno. In the past the only source was rainwater collection, which is challenged by the distinct wet and dry seasons. Most businesses on the island rely on untreated well water, which can be used only for washing and restroom facilities.

The main source of potable water is the Aqua brand 21-liter bottled water, transported from the larger island of Lombok, 6.5 kilometers east of Gili Meno. The bottles are packed onto flat wooden boats and transported from the Pemenang coast of Lombok to Gili Meno, then loaded onto pony carts for local delivery. Owned by French company Danone, Aqua accounts for 60 percent of all bottled-water sales in Indonesia, which in turn requires an intensive plastic recycling infrastructure to clean up the waste.

WATER INFRASTRUCTURE IN HOTEL MODELS

Water consumption in beach resorts is always higher than at inland hotels. Resorts offer many facilities that require large amounts of fresh water, such as swimming pools, Jacuzzis, laundry, and vast gardens and landscapes. A study conducted by the Cornell Hotel Sustainability Benchmarking Index, including more than 10,000 properties and 448 geographies, found the following:

Water benchmark for tropical climate:
638 liters/room night (Low)
2,000 liters/room night (Mid)
4,000 liters/room (High)

Water infrastructure and transport in Gili Meno

Energy Infrastructure

In 2012 the state power company, PLN, connected the power grid of Gili Meno by underwater cable to a plant at the northernmost tip of Lombok that provides a steady supply of 20 kV. Previously a 1.5 MW diesel-fueled generator on Gili Trawangan, the largest island in the archipelago, supplied the three islands—with 350 kW to Gili Air and 170 kW to Gili Meno—via a large underwater cable built in the 1990s. PLN installed 200 solar panels on Gili Trawangan as a backup power supply; three solar power plants on the Gili islands provide a total of 800 kW. Karma Reef resort has its own diesel generator for events and emergencies. Today the power system on Lombok is based almost entirely on fossil fuels, mainly diesel, followed by coal. Hydropower and solar energy complete the current power supply.

The Greenpark Resort (2002)

Concentrated apartment style and bungalows with split air-conditioning

194 rooms with 24,706 m^2 usable space

8,327 m^2 air-conditioned space (33.71%)

Annual consumption: 748,836 kWh (60%) = 89.92 kWh/m^2

Total: 1,246,326 kWh

Ravindra Beach Resort and Spa (2003)

Concentrated apartment style with central air-conditioning

277 rooms with 34,878 m^2 usable space (40% more rooms)

17,364 m^2 air-conditioned space (49.78%)

Annual consumption: 1,256,540 kWh (34%) = 72 kWh/m^2

Total: 3,643,737 kWh

Food Waste

Built in 2016, the recycling station on Gili Trawangan collects 10 to 15 tons of recyclable waste (plastic bottles, cans, glass bottles, and milk cartons) every ten days and transports it off Gili Meno to a recycling station in Lombok. The island produces a daily average of 8.8 tons (8,800 kg) of waste, of which 49 percent is organic. Only 230 kg of organic waste is recycled, and of the 72 percent of non-organic recyclable materials, only 28 percent is recycled.

LEFT: Energy infrastructure in Gili Meno

MIDDLE AND RIGHT: Food waste

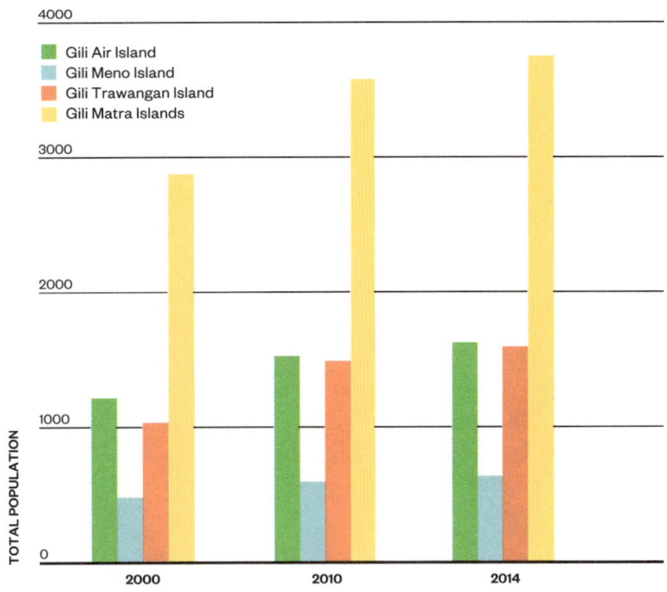

Growth of Tourist Arrivals in the Gili Islands from 2009 to 2014

The Gili Islands have experienced a massive increase in the number of tourists. Gili Meno alone has had an almost tenfold increase, from about 3,900 guests in 2010 to nearly 36,000 in 2014. During this time the islands had a total increase in tourist population from almost 55,000 in 2010 to 437,000 in 2014. The island's interior development increased accordingly in large tourist centers on Gili Trawangan and Gili Air.

Gili Meno Local Population Growth in 2000, 2010, and 2014

While the tourism industry and influx increased rapidly, the number of local residents remained fairly consistent during the four years studied. Gili Meno's population has increased only by 66 residents, from 485 in 2000 to 551 in 2014. The total Gili Island population rose by 1,693, from 2,013 in 2000 to 3,706 in 2014.

Tourism across the Gili Islands

The center of Gili Meno attracts birdwatchers; the east and northwest coasts are popular with sunbathers, the east and west coasts for snorkeling, canoeing, and diving in deeper waters. Surfing is popular south of Gili Trawangan, and fishing southwest of Gili Meno. On Gili Trawangan tourism is centered on the northeast coast, with glass-bottom boat trips, sunbathing, snorkeling, and canoeing. Tourism on Gili Air is based around Karang Petang, on the southeastern corner of the island, for snorkeling and canoeing.

TOP RIGHT: Growth of Tourist Arrivals in the Gili Islands from 2009 to 2014

BOTTOM RIGHT: Tourism across the Gili Islands

OPPOSITE: Gili Meno Local Population Growth in 2000, 2010, and 2014

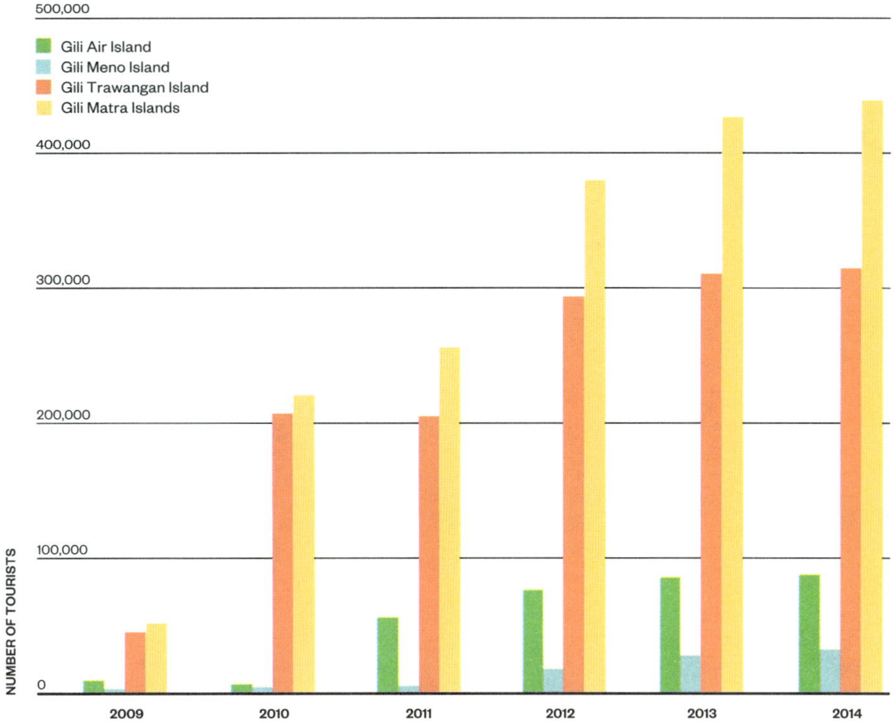

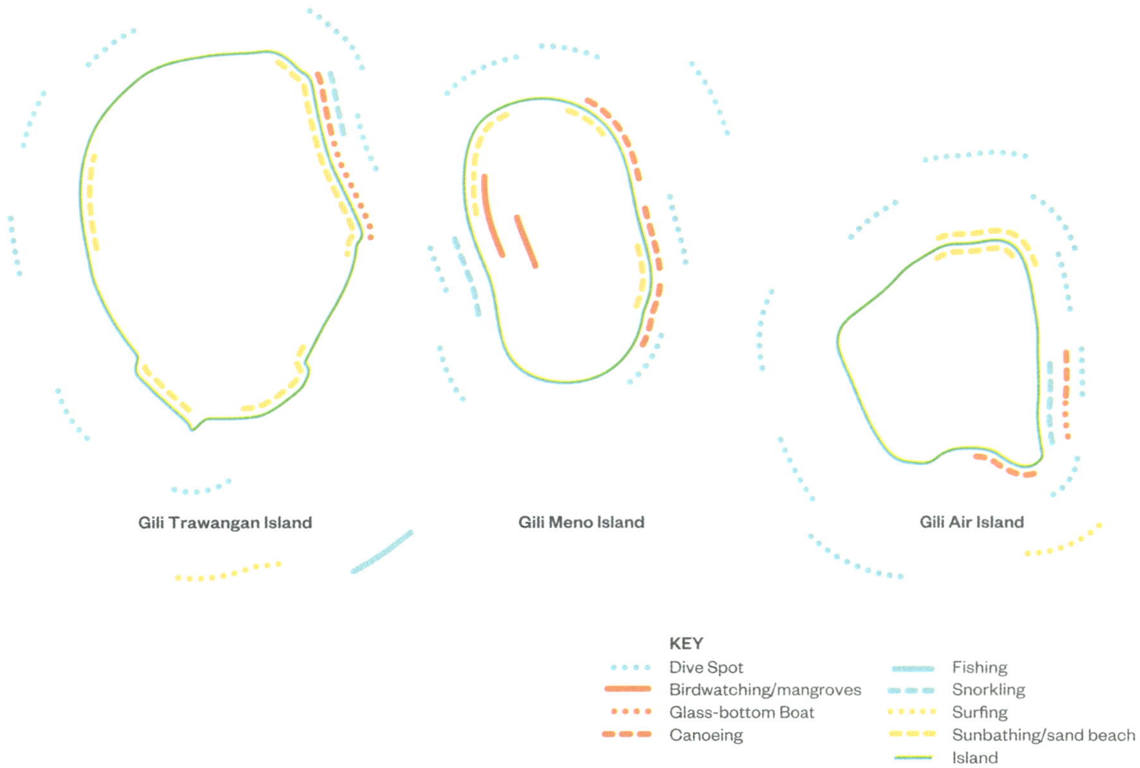

Bamboo and timber clad pavilion

NEW AND LOCAL MATERIALS RESEARCH

Bamboo

A fast-growing, quickly maturing, high-productivity, high-strength, inexpensive, and permanently available local material

A sustainable indigenous building material used for veneers, flooring, scaffolding, furniture, columns, beams, and roofs, bamboo creates a thermally comfortable interior environment in hot-and-humid climate conditions. Depending on where and in what kind of soil it is planted, different species can become fully mature in two to three years in various shades of black, yellow, white, and green. This variation in pigment reflects differing strengths and qualities, which is dependent on the solid exterior culm wall, the bamboo stock. Thus the bamboo is treated to repel insects from burrowing inside and fungi from growing on its surface by soaking it in a saline solution to draw out moisture and infuse it with salt. As bamboo grows in nodes and is not hollow all the way through the interior of a stock, it is often split and shaped into roof shingles, sliced and woven into panels called bedge, or shredded to make the rope used to tie joints and thatching together during construction. Strong when compressed, bamboo makes excellent structural systems.

Alila Villas Uluwatu

In 2005 Singapore architecture firm WOHA designed Alila Villas Uluwatu, which opened in 2009. Located on the dry savannah of Bali's Bukit Peninsula, it comprises a 55-suite hotel with 35 residential villas. The design combines traditional Balinese bamboo architecture and rural landscapes with modern materials. WOHA designed the residential villas as pavilions linked by bridges over water gardens tucked into the hillside terraces. Recycled and sourced locally, the materials include stones from road cuttings, timber repurposed from ironwood railway sleepers acquired at auction. A screen wall composed of salvaged copper batik stamps showcases this traditional craft; local craftspeople made the hotel's furniture, lamps, and accessories.

LEFT: Alila Villas Uluwatu, by WOHA Architects

BELLOW: Bamboo and timber cladding detail

Lava Rock Construction

A local Balinese mixture of sand and broken river pebbles, raw limestone, or lava rocks

The island is formed with many kinds of stone used for building by the Balinese, with heavier materials employed at the structure's base, graduating up to finer materials. The most common stone is metamorphic, such as lava rocks extracted at a rivers' edge or found in riverbeds during the dry season. Often used for ramps, pavilion bases, gates, and courtyard walls, the black lava stones have tiny holes that help to regulate heat gain and provide traction on terraces and landscaped pathways.

TOP: Lava rock wall foundation

BOTTOM: Lava rock interior wall structure

SANGKAR
RESTAURANT

Bulgari Hotels and Resorts, by Antonio Citterio Patricia Viel (ACPV)

Bulgari Hotels and Resorts

In 2006 the architecture firm Antonio Citterio Patricia Viel and Partners designed the Bulgari Hotels and Resorts in Bali on 8.4 hectares. The spatial organization of the resort provides for quiet private spaces for the residential areas on the western side with screened views. Public spaces on the eastern side of the resort are organized around an artificial lake, with open-air bars on the edge of a cliff. The sharply sloping coast required complex terracing with volcanic rocks that make up the interior walls. The material fits perfectly into the dark gray stone of the landscape, which recalls a walled medieval village. Yet here views are characterized by tropical vegetation growing in private gardens and the roofs of Bali's resort skyline, composed of alang-alang, a straw obtained from the leaves of coconut trees.

Limestone (Palimanan)

A local Javanese rock created from ancient marine life such as coral and mollusk

Limestone is composed of the fragmented remains of ancient marine organisms found along the coastline. Lightweight, soft, and easy to work with, it is often used in facade cladding or as tiles. Paras, or volcanic tuffs, are sedimentary rocks similar to sandstone whose weathering evokes older structures in Indonesia. Limestone is also more readily available and less expensive than other types of stone, making it cost effective.

Uluwatu, by SAOTA

In 2018 SAOTA architects reinterpreted the distinctive vernacular timber pavilions of Bali in an Uluwatu retreat. The architects designed a house on a limestone cliff oriented east–west, facing the ocean on the east. The site's scale accommodates a resort-inspired layout with separate suites and living spaces in a fragmented arrangement that integrates indoor and outdoor spaces. A series of courtyards, gardens, and planted terraces are woven into the architecture, combining the architectural structure and planting with the existing rocky, overgrown landscape. Throughout the resort a concrete texture and natural finishes such as local stone are overlaid with timberwork. Vertical screens, joinery, and decorative metalwork, such as the faceted bronze aluminum behind the bar and in the cigar lounge, enrich the materiality. Glass curtain walls and the lightweight local timber roofs with board-marked concrete seem to float above the villas. The sloping roof responds to the east–west orientation of the house, inviting in the morning light and opening up to ocean views while providing shelter from the harsh afternoon light from the west and the inclement rain showers typical of Bali.

ABOVE: Uluwatu, by SAOTA

LEFT: Limestone interior wall structure and floor cladding

OPPOSITE: Limestone terrace and cliffs

Bioplastics

Plastics produced from renewable biomass sources

Globally we produce roughly 310 million tons of plastic each year, half of which are assumed to be single use, an amount expected to quadruple by 2050. Instead 90 percent of plastics could be derived from plants or other renewable materials as bioplastics to reduce emissions and sequester carbon. Technical advantages include thermal properties ideal for 3-D printing. However, bioplastic cannot be composted unless separated from other plastics: without source separation and appropriate processing the material is "all dressed up with nowhere to go" in most municipal waste streams—except to the landfills.

3-D Printed Urban Cabin, by DUS Architects

DUS Architects designed the Urban Cabin for a park in the formerly industrial center of Amsterdam in 2016. The cabin is 3-D printed with a black bio-based material that showcases different types of facade ornament, form-optimization techniques, and innovative solutions for insulation and material consumption. The floor and stepped porch are combined with a concrete finish creating a pattern that extends into a pocket park. In the green space around the house there is a sculptural outdoor 3-D-printed bathtub. Being built of bioplastics allows for the material from the Urban Cabin to be reused and recycled over time.

ABOVE: The 3-D Printed Urban Cabin, by DUS Architects

OPPOSITE LEFT: Tessellated bioplastic wall

OPPOSITE RIGHT: Bioplastic wall and window detail

STUDIO BRIEF

THE YALE STUDIO: *GILI MENO*

The professors asked students to design a new resort typology as a prototype for the future of global sustainable tourism. The concept entailed a waterfront vacation site built with minimal environmental impact in construction and operation, as a viable tourist destination to enhance the local economy. The programs of the diverse resort models the students developed in the studio responded to the selection of an ideal tourist demographic. At the beginning of the semester two initial types were defined—the luxury vacationer seeking rest and relaxation with wellness, sports, and fine dining facilities, and the millennial backpacker seeking a more rugged and communal travel experience with activities centered around social interaction. Guided by John Spence, students worked toward defining a program that would be efficient in organization for staff, commercially viable for stakeholders, and appropriate for the chosen demographic. Patrick Bellew assisted the students in developing a unique approach to environmental design and sustainable development. Henry Squire, along with Tim Newton, provided the weekly critique needed to refine the programs and schemes over the course of the semester. The outcome of the studio was a master plan focused on the desired resort clientele, with additional thematic programs, all with a strong emphasis on sustainability. The additional creation of complementary physical models, section drawings,

View of the site toward former coconut plantation

renderings, animations, or plan drawings was up to the discretion of the student to better complement their individual schemes.

The site is located on the east coast of Gili Meno, at the center of the Gili archipelago 6.5 km off the west coast of Lombok, the largest island east of Bali, Indonesia. Until World War II Gili Meno had no human inhabitants because the island lacked freshwater sources; sparse tropical forests covered the inland, and mangroves grew along the coast. The Japanese had built a bunker and prisoner-of-war camp after the invasion of Dutch Indonesia during the war. After the independence of Indonesia, fishermen from Lombok began to settle the island as a fishing outpost. Simultaneously the local government established a coconut plantation farmed by inmates from Lombok prisons; the project was abandoned by the 1980s. Around that time tourists discovered the Gili Islands, first Gili Air, the smallest island with the largest population, and then Gili Meno, the central island, and finally Gili Trawangan, the largest island. Due to the lack of human habitation for so long, the Gili Islands became known for untouched coral reefs, fantastic dive sites, and rich fishing spots. The resort and service industries are the largest employers on Gili Meno today, along with a local fishing industry. As the tourism sector has grown on the islands over the past 40 years, so has the negative impact on the ecosystem. Many fishermen now use dynamite and cyanide to make larger catches, which kills species of tropical fish, sea turtles, mollusks, and seaweed. With damage to the local ecosystem, the coral reefs and mangroves surrounding the islands are also slowly dying. Excess nonbiodegradable waste abounds, including glass and plastic bottles, cardboard shipping boxes, and aluminum soda and alcohol cans. Global warming, sea-level rise, and an increase in natural disasters have become a serious issue for these low-lying islands. The 4,500 local inhabitants—totaling 500 on Gili Meno and 2,000 each on Gili Trawangan and Gili Air—are either the descendants of the fishermen who settled the island from nearby Lombok or migrants who work for the many resorts, dive centers, and fishing companies during the week and return home to Lombok on weekends.

EXCESS NONBIODE-GRADABLE WASTE ABOUNDS, INCLUDING GLASS AND PLASTIC BOTTLES, CARDBOARD SHIPPING BOXES, AND ALUMINUM SODA AND ALCOHOL CANS.

ABOVE: Local village on Gili Meno near the site

OPPOSITE: Accessing the growth of bamboo shoots

The studio site on Gili Meno encompasses approximately 5.2 hectares with 180 meters of eastern beach frontage extending 320 meters inland and 200 meters out and over the sea. Four hectares is to be developed into a resort program and the remaining 1.2 hectares, at the southwestern corner of the site, will be adapted for a local communal program. Of those 4 hectares only about 1.15 total hectares of the site could be built on for the resort. This is broken down as .175 hectares for circulation space, .25 hectares for front of house, .45 hectares for rooms, .12 hectares for support spaces and .15 hectares for staff accommodations. Incorporating these flexible programs, the students reshaped the site to create a next-generation resort model that could tackle the existing environmental degradation caused by the resort industry and issues related to the procurement of clean drinking water, renewable energy, and fresh food.

The front-of-house common areas had to accommodate varying traveler demographics. The programs included restaurants, resort and beach bars, workout spaces, wellness centers, game rooms, a dive center, libraries, an entrance lobby, and bike parking. For back-of-house staff areas the students considered service functions, offices, luggage rooms, laundry, staff kitchens, food storage and pantries, gardener's huts, and maintenance for electrical generators and HVAC. Energy centers, water storage, and waste recycling were major sustainable aspects to be developed as well. Ecological features related to community land use included facilities for food production, fish farms, community centers to promote interaction between guests and locals, solar farming areas to generate power, algae farms, wind farms, tidal energy generators, and

OPPOSITE: Students creating models to test the building of bamboo structures

recycling hubs to handle waste from the resort and island as a whole. Ecological resilience is a key consideration in the project, and the programs provide spaces of refuge for guests in the event of a tsunami or earthquake, like the one that struck the islands in summer 2018. These provisions were identified and designed with suitable elevation, construction materials, and resilience features that ensure passive and active strategies to protect guests, staff, and local residents on the island in the short and long term.

THE STUDENTS ASPIRED FOR THE NEW RESORT TO BE A NATURAL EXTENSION OF THE TERRAIN, CLIMATE, AND CULTURAL LANDSCAPE.

The Karma Reef resort is located on the site, a low-lying island in the tropics that is often hit by major natural disasters. Monsoons and rising sea levels spurred by climate change, as well as powerful earthquakes and tsunamis, are serious issues. The professors encouraged students to research and propose novel methods of environmental design employing biomimicry and new green technologies. The indigenous methods and materials used in vernacular Indonesian architecture inspired the students after their visit to the Green School, designed by John Hardy and his daughter, Elora Hardy, of IBUKU. The students met with the workers who treat, prepare, and build bamboo, including carpenter Jörg Stamm and artist Aldo Landwehr. The students aspired for the new resort to be a natural extension of the terrain, climate, and cultural landscape.

Throughout the semester the students became more grounded in the commercial reality of this resort typology and its ecological considerations. Going into midterm they were asked to organize a narrative around the ideal traveler's arrival on the island and what they would expect to experience at the resort. The architecture and sustainable components of the projects would naturally unfold and be revealed through the design narrative. Engineers, interior designers, resort staff, and architects joined the studio reviews to allow for diverse feedback. The results were seen in projects that proposed building in the ocean and using the motion of the waves to capture energy, the creation of electrified models on the seabed to repopulate coral, and the use of electric battery cells to make the island energy supply more self-sufficient. For the final studio project the professors asked each student to create more detailed concepts in terms of a specific commercial or ecological aspect.

The final projects adapted a series of approaches, ranging from luxury family resorts that reflected local Indonesian design and romantic backpacker villages for single travelers to projects that devised the resort as an ecological machine to combat climate change. Students presented the projects in different media, such as bamboo models to test the structural design feasibility, graphics animating worker and guest movement through the site, and diagrams illustrating ecological design features such as rainwater gardens. At the end of the semester each student incorporated aspects of sustainable design, resort typology, and ecological materiality into a vision for a next-generation model of tourism.

OPPOSITE: Looking up through the lightwell of a parametric bamboo building at the Green School, Bali

Parabolic bamboo roof construction

STUDIO PROJECTS

NEW MODELS OF TOURISM

Today's younger generation wants a unique experience that often does not fit into any standard model of holiday. These projects propose new methods for guests seeking to experience romance on a tropical island, attend a festival for the creative arts, or blend play and remote work from a tropical island.

Throughout the course of the studio, Patrick Bellew directed students in their proposals for ecological strategies, sustainable materials, and climate-intuitive design concepts suited to the local ecosystem of Gili Meno. He guided students in finding the best ways to shape bamboo structures for use in traditional passive systems of heating and cooling, such as roofs and rooms oriented toward coastal breezes, to moderate temperatures in the hotel suites. He also introduced new active technologies, such as the integration of solar panels and wave power systems, to provide sustainable energy generation for the island. Bellew demonstrated his representation and illustrative skills, developed over three decades at Atelier Ten, to show students how the complex climate systems could be depicted simply in architectural drawings and models.

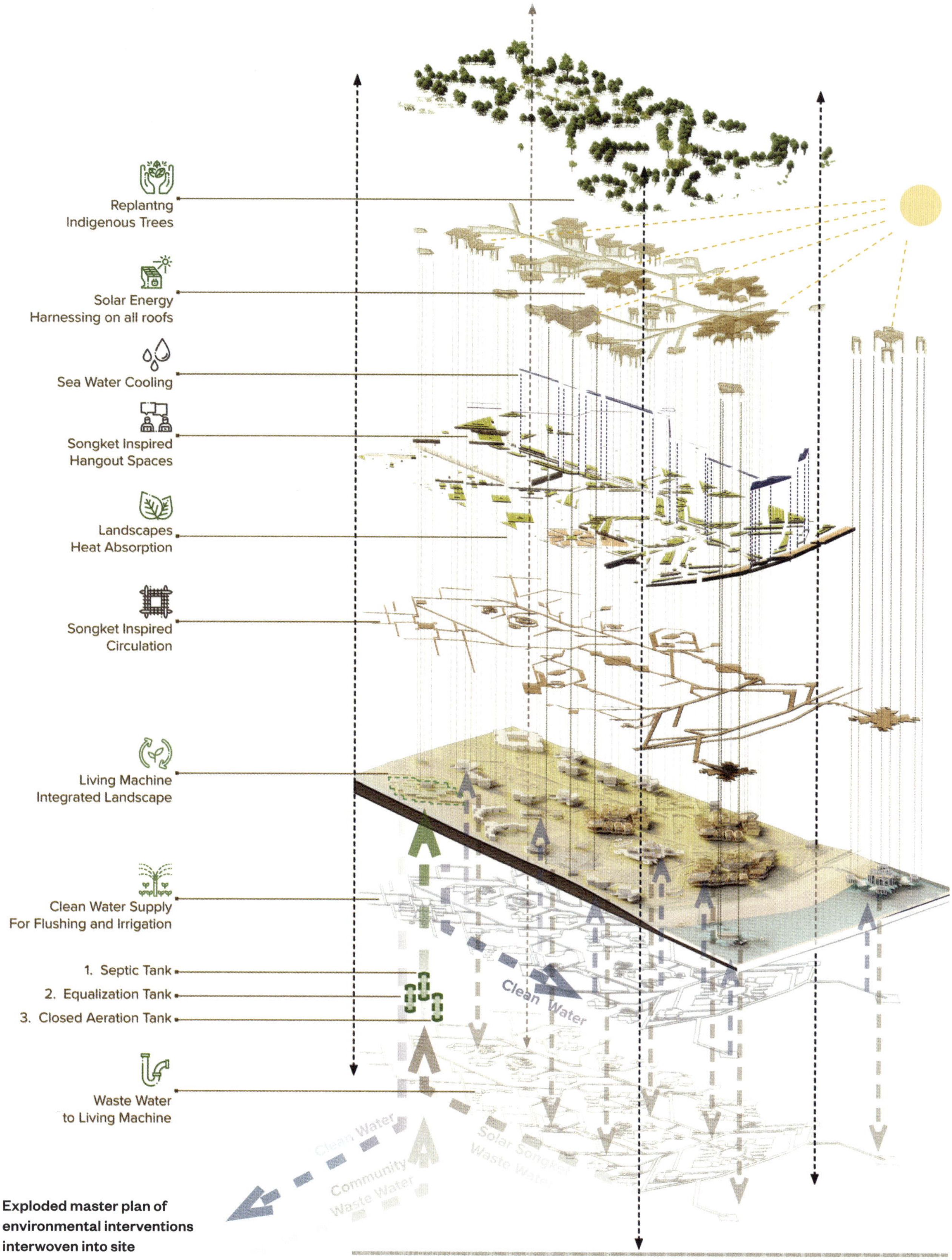

Exploded master plan of environmental interventions interwoven into site

Justin Tsang
Solar Songket

Solar Songket is an environmentally and socially integrated play-and-work lifestyle resort inspired by the local Indonesian textile *songket*. This fabric takes time to create and is never completed alone. It is a vital representation of collaboration, a correlation of the millennial generation who would come to the resort and not work by confined hours and spaces. One-quarter of the world's population is currently composed of millennials and constitutes up to 50 percent of the workforce. Resorts balancing work and life are rising fast in Indonesia, Thailand, and Vietnam.

Solar Songket offers an interwoven eco-community experience divided into three elements: playing hard in search of meaningful discoveries; working hard yet not confined by standard frameworks; appreciating life through travel that benefits the environment, health, and society.

The Solar Songket motif is configured in accordance with site conditions including the prevailing wind, sun path, terrain, and sea. Every faceted roof exposed to the sun is photovoltaic, with irrigation and ventilation systems embedded in the structures. Albeit hidden, such a circular system integrated the intricate engineering as part of the motto of Solar Songket.

TOP: Sectional model of restaurant, back

BOTTOM: Sectional model of restaurant with environmental interventions, front

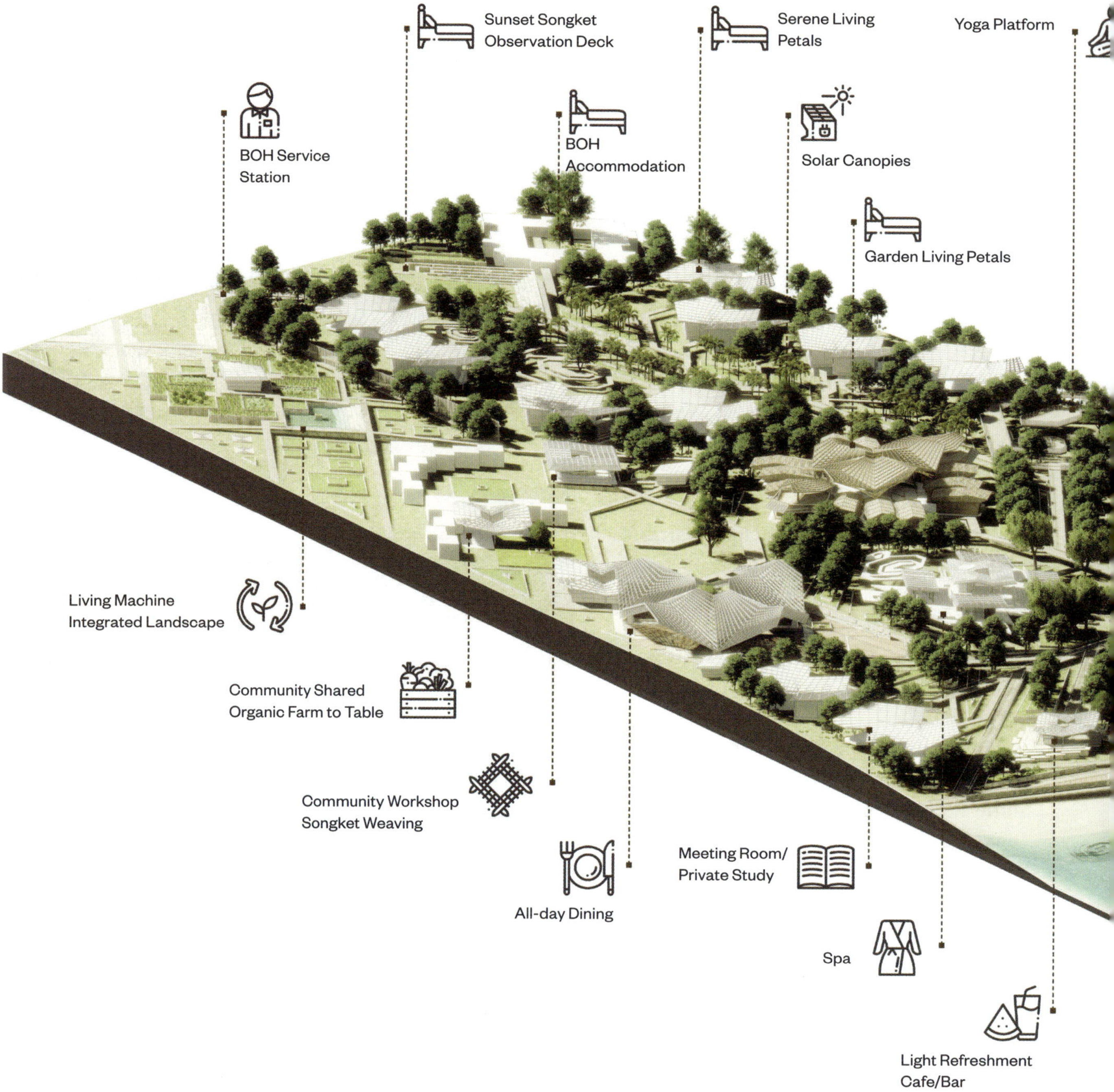

Sunset Songket Observation Deck
Serene Living Petals
Yoga Platform
BOH Service Station
BOH Accommodation
Solar Canopies
Garden Living Petals
Living Machine Integrated Landscape
Community Shared Organic Farm to Table
Community Workshop Songket Weaving
All-day Dining
Meeting Room/ Private Study
Spa
Light Refreshment Cafe/Bar

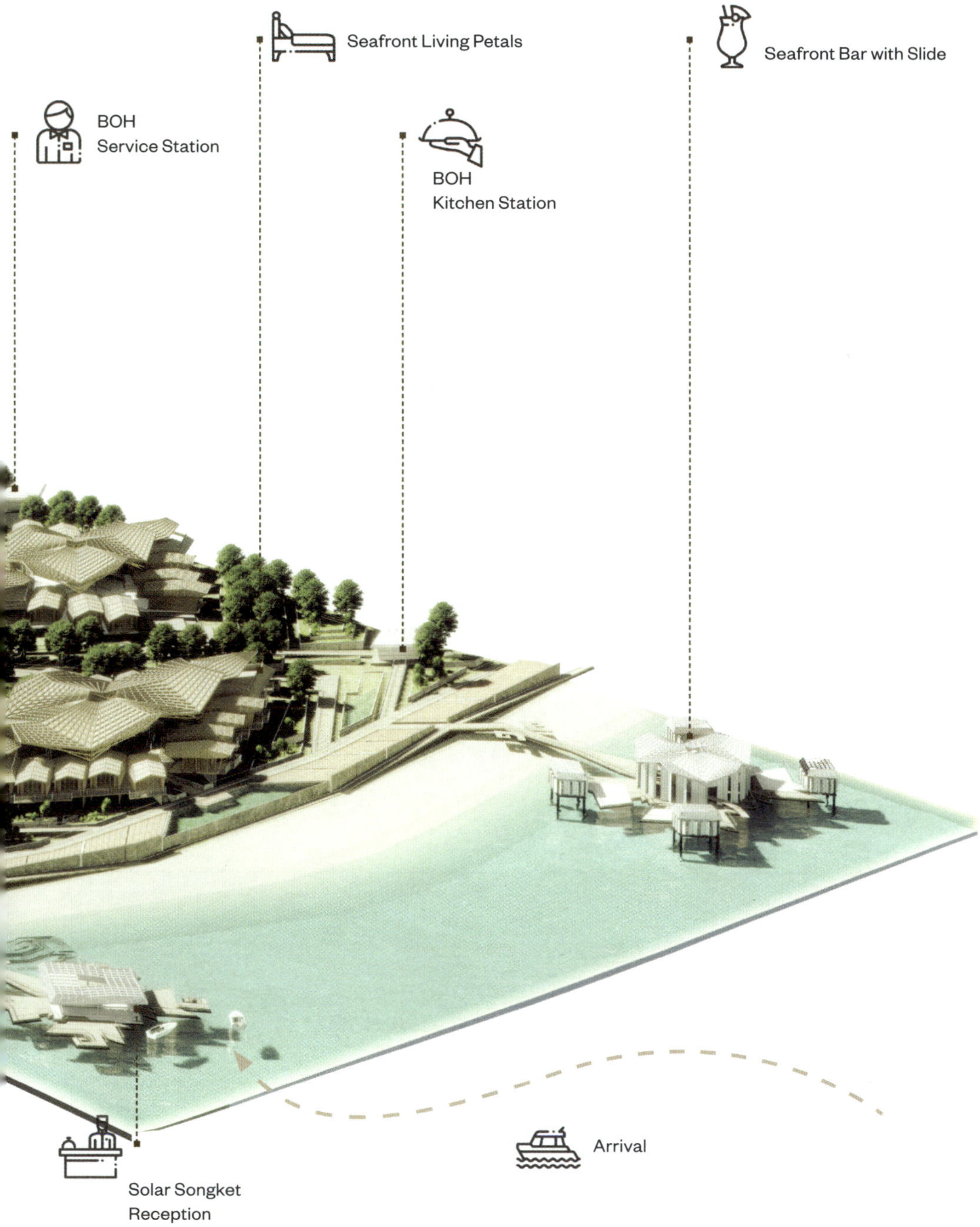

Axon of master plan with eco-community laid out across the site

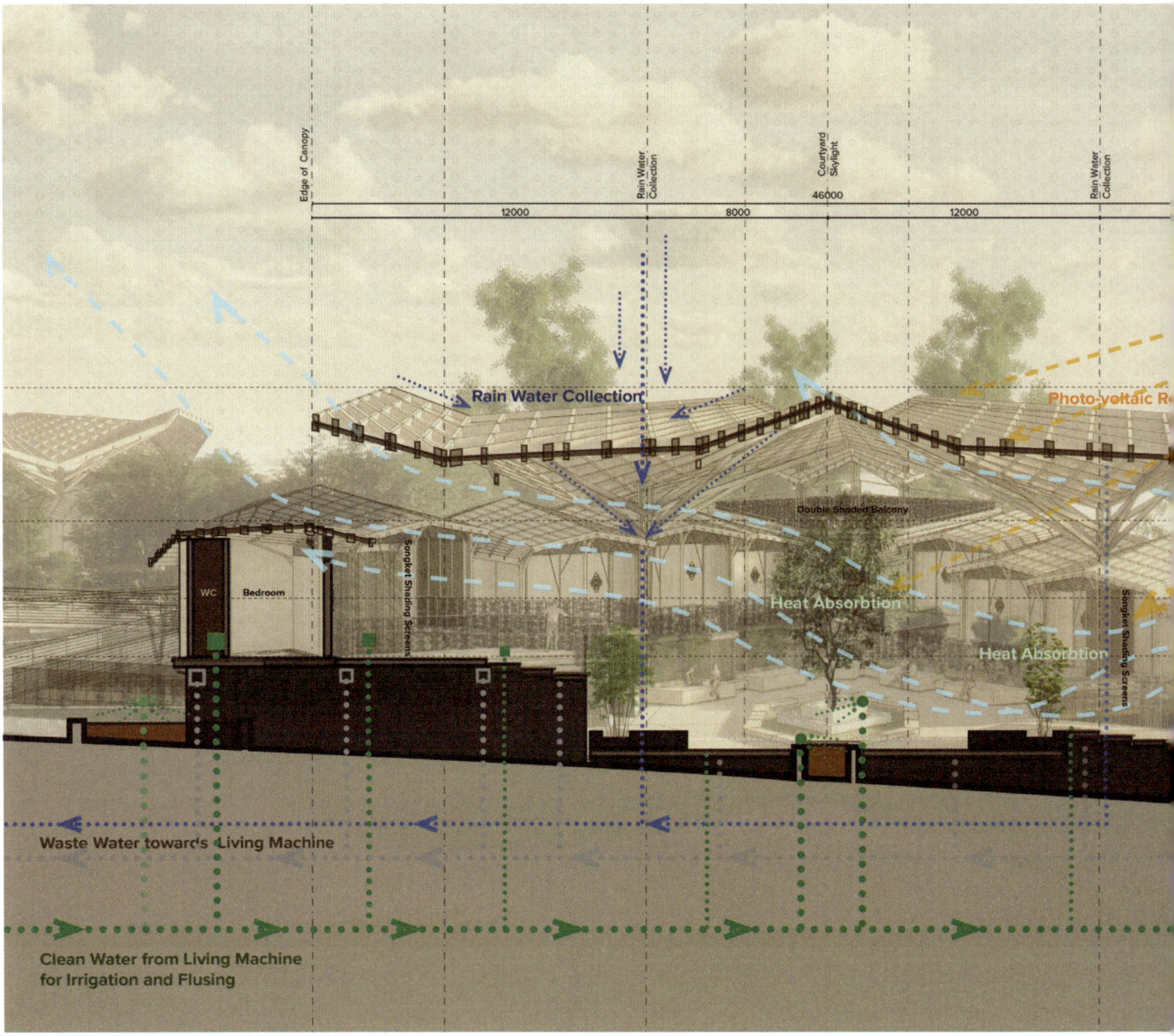

The coworking-and-living model at Solar Songket is environmentally interwoven with local craft workshops and traditional culinary exchanges as part of daily operation. Solar Songket reinforces relationships between vacationers and local neighborhoods through the environmentally integrated architecture and landscapes that harness energy for its electrical demands. The resort welcomes "working holidaymakers" to mingle holistically with guests as they participate in events and workshops. Therefore Solar Songket mixes the play-and-work lifestyle with a unique guest experience.

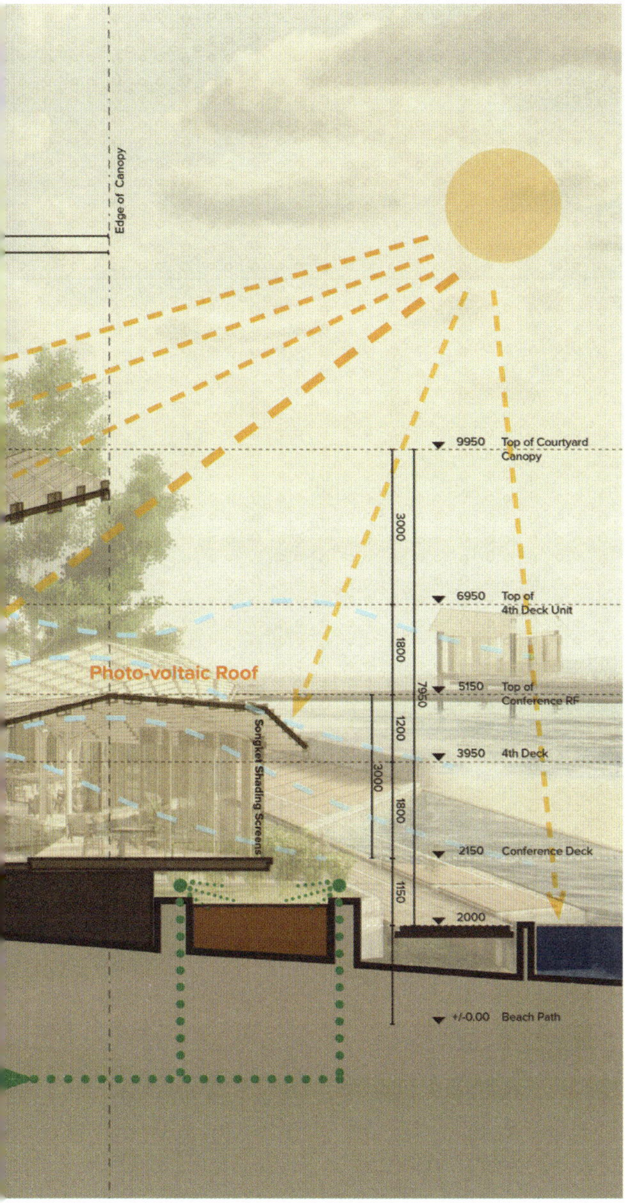

LEFT: Section of restaurant with overlaid environmental interventions

RIGHT: View looking across the site from the spa toward the restaurant and the sea relationships

Smit Patel
Gili Cinta

Gili Cinta translates into English as "Love Island." The secluded beaches of Gili Meno make for an extremely intimate experience and the perfect romantic walk. The master plan is an extension of this walk from the beach to the island interior, encountering the different landscapes. The resort is a choreographed set of scenes that maximizes interaction between the guests in the hope of finding the perfect date. The restaurant and bar set the stage, revealing interactions in modular tiers due to the remote nature and ecological demands of the island.

The hostel occupies a more intimate part of the site and is laid out in a circular radius with vegetable gardens around a central barbecue pit, providing food for the restaurant. For a first date one might pick vegetables and cook a meal with the help of a chef, pick flowers to bring to an incense-making workshop, or attend one of the Canang Sari Workshops. Amid coconut trees and along the coast, clusters of premium rooms or "Love Nests" provide partners an escape from the communal experience. The Love Nests are oriented for views of sunrise and sunset.

The resort views sustainability as an integral part of the dating experience and relies on passive systems to reduce energy consumption. The waste-management systems coordinate the demand of the island. The resort acknowledges the importance of sustainability among young travelers by involving guests in the regeneration of island ecology.

ABOVE: Rendered axon of bamboo restaurant module

OPPOSITE: View of Love Nests in the sky

Land Love Nests

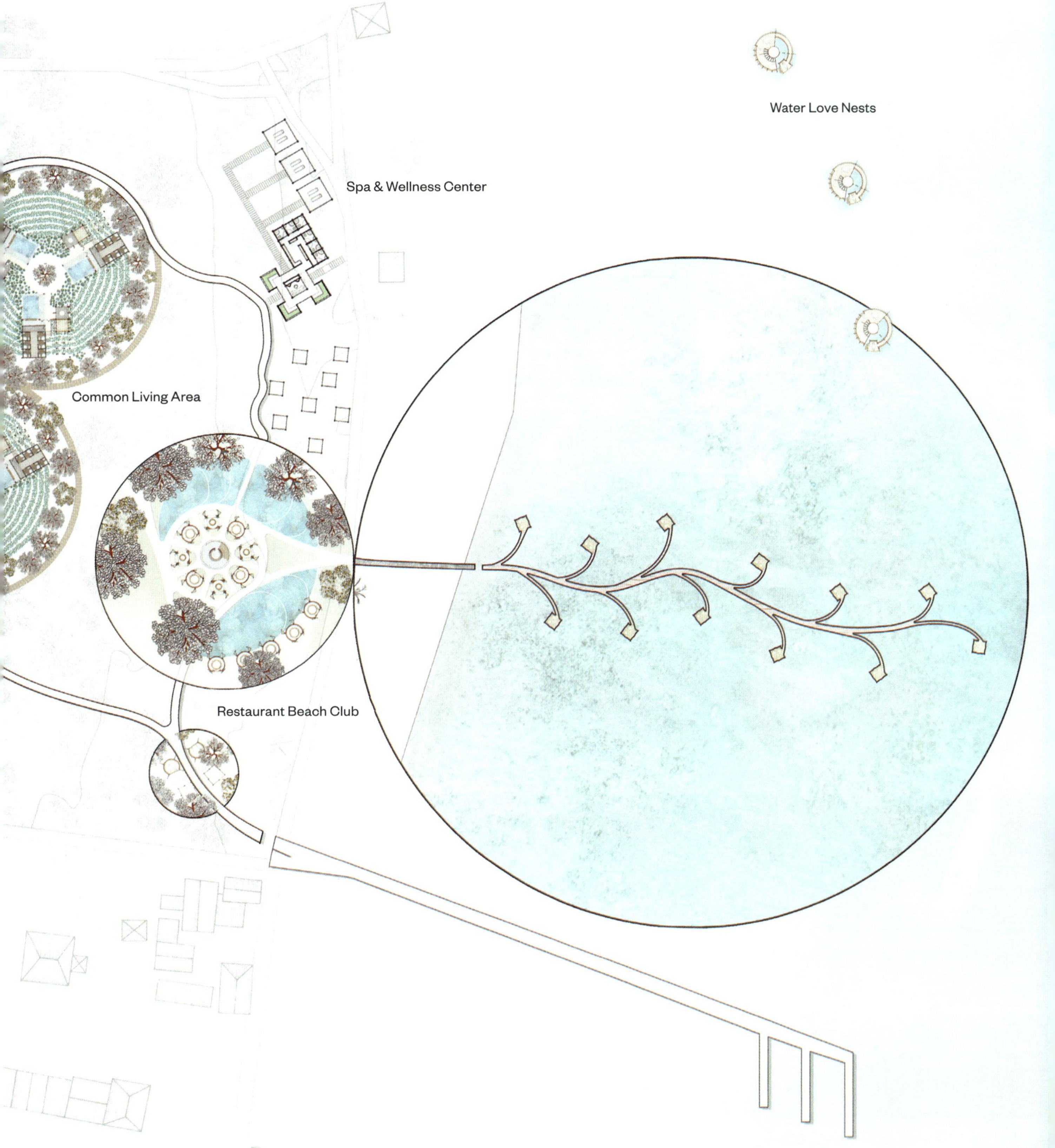

Master plan with labeled zones and site features

ABOVE: View of restaurant and pool out to the sea

FAR LEFT: Ecological aggregation of hostel units

LEFT: Reception floor plan

Anna Borou Yu
PARK (Performance Art Resort of Karma)

The PARK (Performance Art Resort of Karma) is a performance art residency and site for an annual festival on Gili Meno. The resort reflects the traditional performance art and culture of Indonesia as well as global art forms. Through engaging in artistic outreach, tourists better understand and appreciate the needs of the local population.

The culture of Indonesia is close to the sea and soil, maritime life and the land. Visitors arrive by boat to the Gili Islands from the Sea Stage, a circular reception center at the edge of a coral reef, where they can watch dancers in an underwater welcome show. Then they proceed to the beach bar and the two performance centers, where they can enjoy traditional food along with vernacular dance and music.

The resort design incorporates a bamboo structure, leaf screens, and solar panels and focuses on three different activities. It works as a performance art residency with villas where 60 guests and artists stay from one week to one month to learn local music and dances and cooperate in a monthly recital. The annual festival welcomes the most experimental performances based on the Indonesian and Southeast Asian culture on its Moonlight Stage, around which 180 backpackers sleep in tents for one week while interacting with villa residents. At other times of the year the back part of the festival grounds is used to grow bananas, generating crops for the local community.

ABOVE: Axon of the PARK resort during the annual festival with the Moonlight Stage, backpacker tents, and Artist Villas

OPPOSITE: Outdoor recital by resident artist at the Performance Center

View of Sea Stage, where visitors can watch the dancers in the underwater welcome show

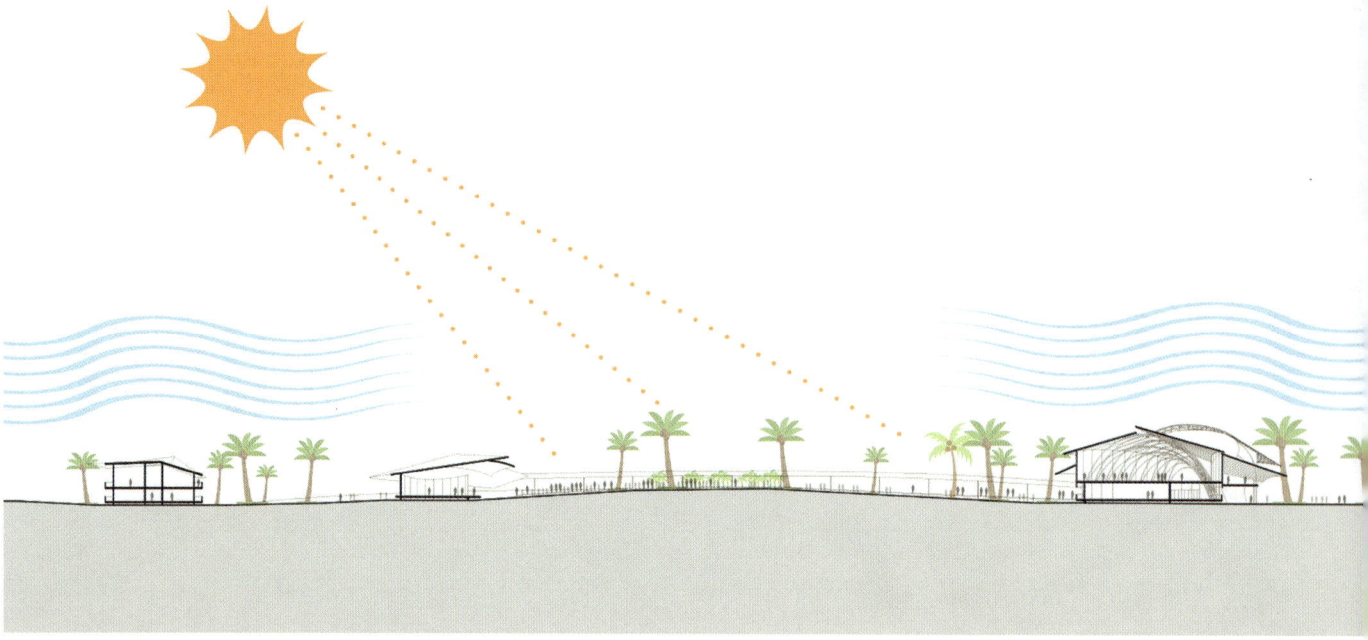

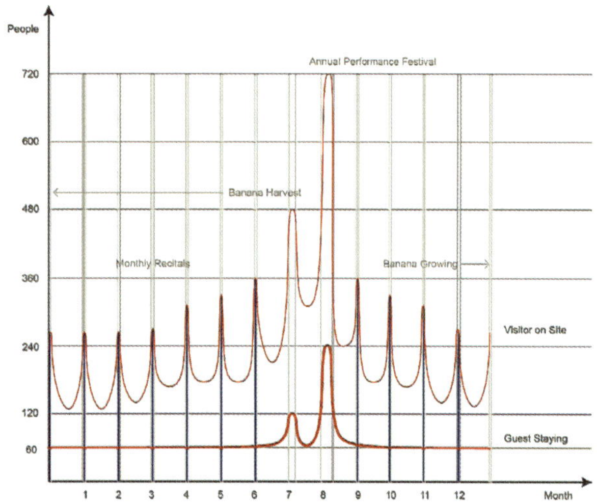

Demographic analysis of PARK throughout a year

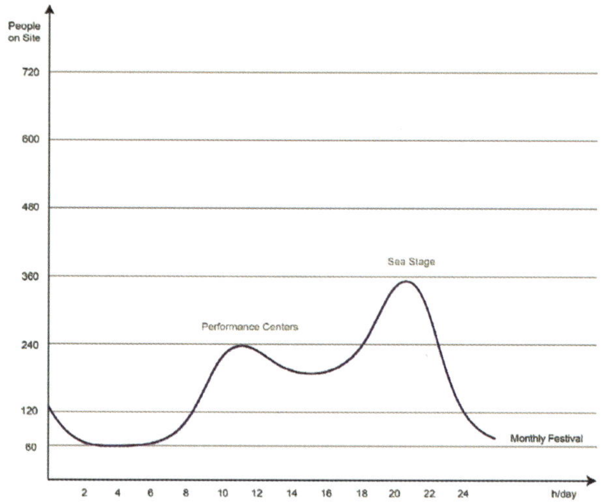

Demographic analysis of PARK throughout a day

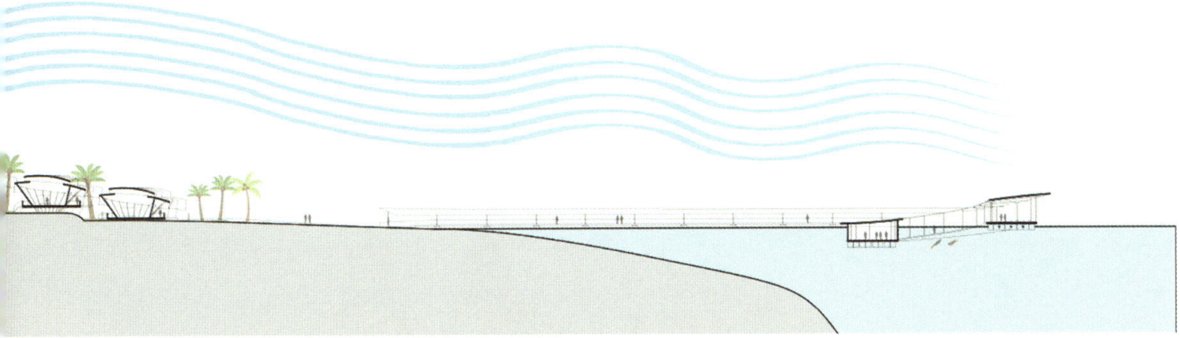

ABOVE: Long section from the Sea Stage, Beach Bar, Artist Villas and the two Performance Centers with solar and wind impact

LEFT TOP: View from Performance Center toward Artist Villas

LEFT BOTTOM: Performance Center at night with traditional Indonesian dance show

OPPOSITE: Yearly schedule of PARK events in relation to the cycle of Banana growing and harvesting

ECOLOGICAL ARCHITECTURE

Emphasizing the ecological impact of the resort, these projects analyzed how architecture can have a positive impact on the local environment, ecosystems, and resort supply chains. The students in this section integrated a greater degree of renewable systems in relation to water, food, and electricity; focused on renewable materials such as local stone and bamboo; and proposed sustainable modular construction methods for resort design.

OPPOSITE: Laélia Kim-Lan Vaulot, view through reception toward seafront villas

Baolin Paul Shen
E^2CO

The hospitality industry is well known as a significant consumer of natural resources, especially water, accounting for approximately 3.4 percent of global domestic water use. Beach hotels and resorts often compete for water with the locals who use it for agriculture. This water stress is exacerbated by the seasonal dry climates of these popular tropical regions.

E^2CO is an environmentally sustainable and socially responsible eco-resort that provides a unique work-live experience for emerging groups of digital and corporate nomads. The resort centers on a concept of ecology, coliving, and coworking where guests are immersed in a series of stunning landscapes. They live in the canopy villages, work in the water garden, stroll along the rain lakes, and wander around the wetland garden. On the south side of the resort is a community garden where the resort guests can interact with locals and engage in their activities.

In addition to creating a delightful environment, these landscapes are designed as systems to harvest and recycle water. The rain garden acts as a sponge that filters and collects rainwater to be stored in the rain lakes, which are stormwater reservoirs. The wetland garden is an ecological sewage-treatment system

TOP: Seawater greenhouse and village community garden

BOTTOM: View from bedroom to beach landscape

OPPOSITE: View of rain garden working space

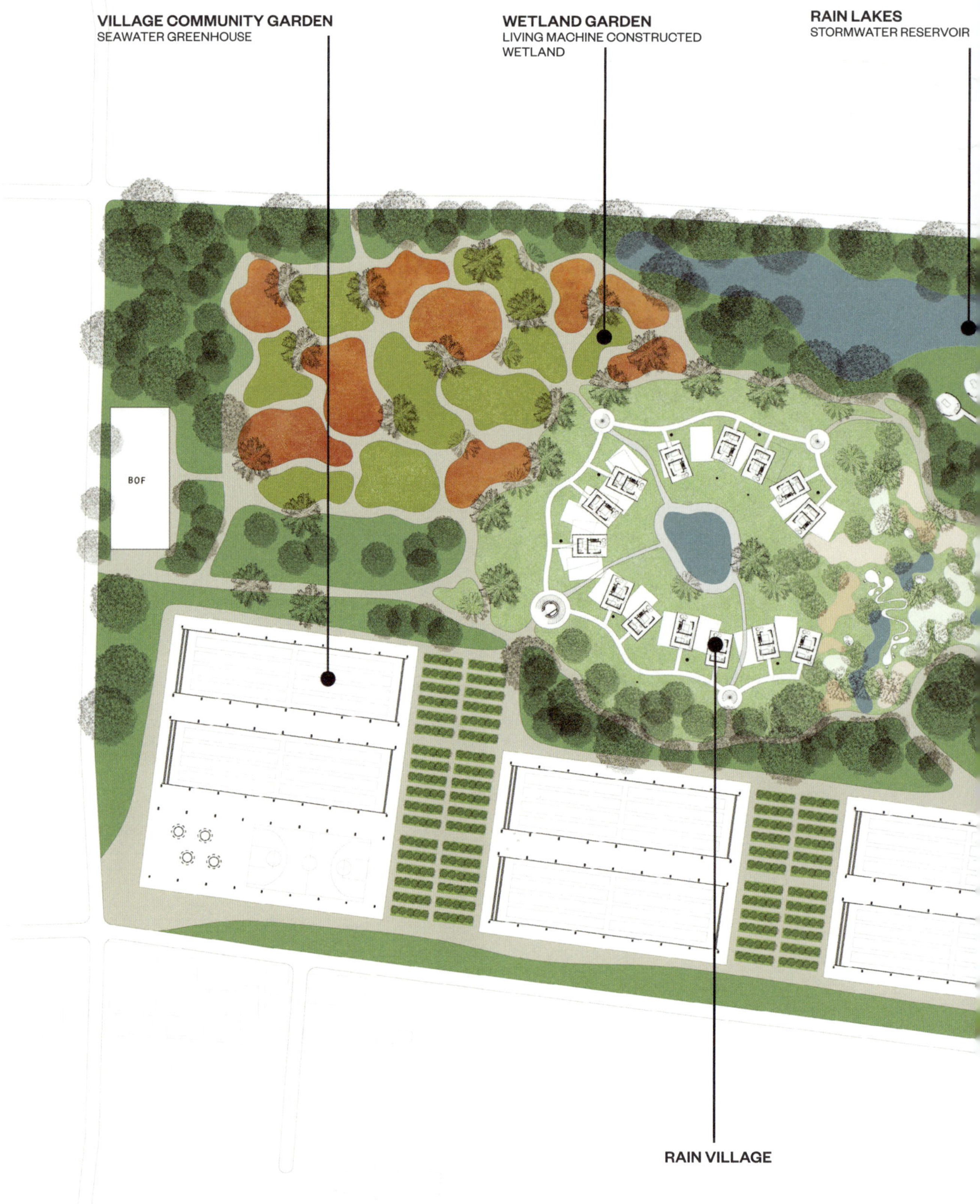
VILLAGE COMMUNITY GARDEN
SEAWATER GREENHOUSE
WETLAND GARDEN
LIVING MACHINE CONSTRUCTED WETLAND
RAIN LAKES
STORMWATER RESERVOIR
BOF
RAIN VILLAGE

E²CO master plan showing the program

that recycles the gray water produced by daily resort operations. The community gardens are seawater greenhouses that aid the production of food with fresh water as excess by-product. Instead of competing for fresh water with locals, E^2CO resort can achieve complete water independence and give back to the community. By staying at the resort, guests will be educated on water issues and encouraged to engage in efforts to contribute to the local community.

ABOVE: View of rain garden

OPPOSITE: Rain garden with diagram of filtering and collection process

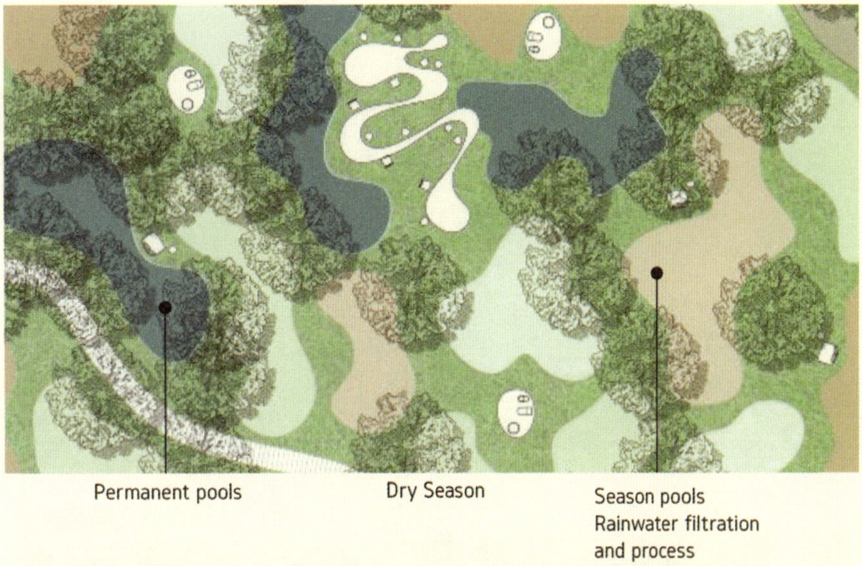
Permanent pools
Dry Season
Season pools
Rainwater filtration
and process

Wet Season

RAIN GARDEN

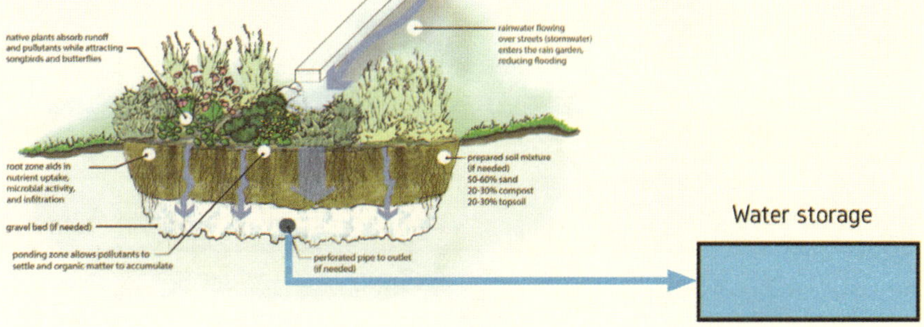
native plants absorb runoff and pollutants while attracting songbirds and butterflies
rainwater flowing over streets (stormwater) enters the rain garden, reducing flooding
root zone aids in nutrient uptake, microbial activity, and infiltration
prepared soil mixture (if needed) 50-60% sand 20-30% compost 20-30% topsoil
gravel bed (if needed)
ponding zone allows pollutants to settle and organic matter to accumulate
perforated pipe to outlet (if needed)
Water storage

Rukshan Eranga Vathupola
Larung

Gili Meno has been deeply intertwined with the growth of international tourism since the 1980s, leading to the development of insular infrastructural systems—clean water procurement, construction material shipment, electricity generation, food production, and waste management—that are heavily dependent on supply chains originating on the mainland. When considering next-generation tourism, efforts must be made to improve outdated environmental cohabitation systems and communal engagement as well as introduce ways for Gili Meno to become self-sufficient.

In response to these conditions, the Larung resort is a machine for environmental restoration that provides a new experience for a generation of eco-conscious travelers. In order to break decades of dependence on distant supply chains, new infrastructure must be built and new systems established to allow the island to thrive. Therefore the resort acts to close loops in the supply chain by generating resources for the island. The resort is divided into four distinct zones, according to the varied local ecologies, to deal more effectively with current issues.

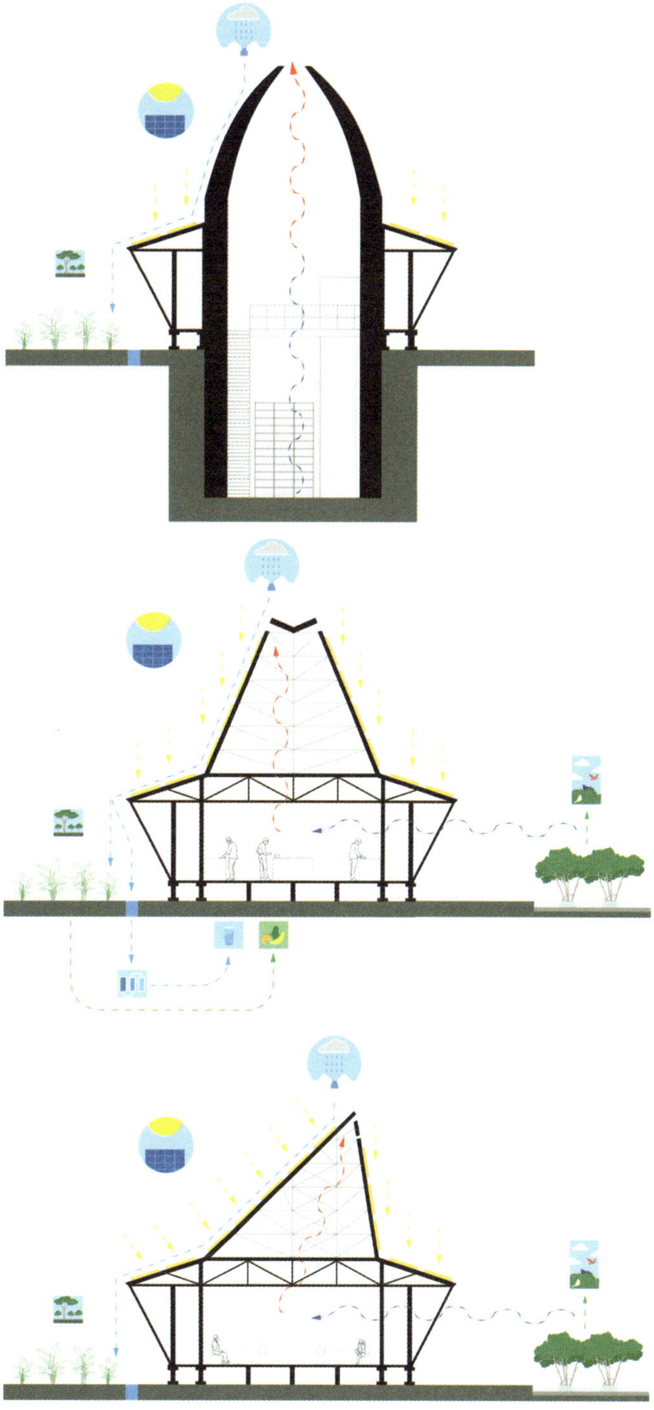

ABOVE: Ecological section of restaurant at three points in relation to mangroves and local crops

OPPOSITE: View toward the sea with the arrival dock, Houseboats, Reception, and Sauna

The four zones are defined as the Sea, the Coast, the Greenery, and the Back of Site. One arrives on the Sea via a houseboat that travels the Indonesian archipelago stopping at different resorts, culminating with its arrival on Gili Meno. The Coast zone hosts the arrival desk, sauna, dive center, and restaurant to the north, along with the spa at the south end of the site. In the Greenery zone larger island villas are surrounded by gardens that grow the food and bamboo used for construction materials for the resort and local community. Finally, at the Back of Site there is modular housing for resort staff.

ABOVE: Larung master plan

OPPOSITE: Section of Houseboat in relation to coral reef

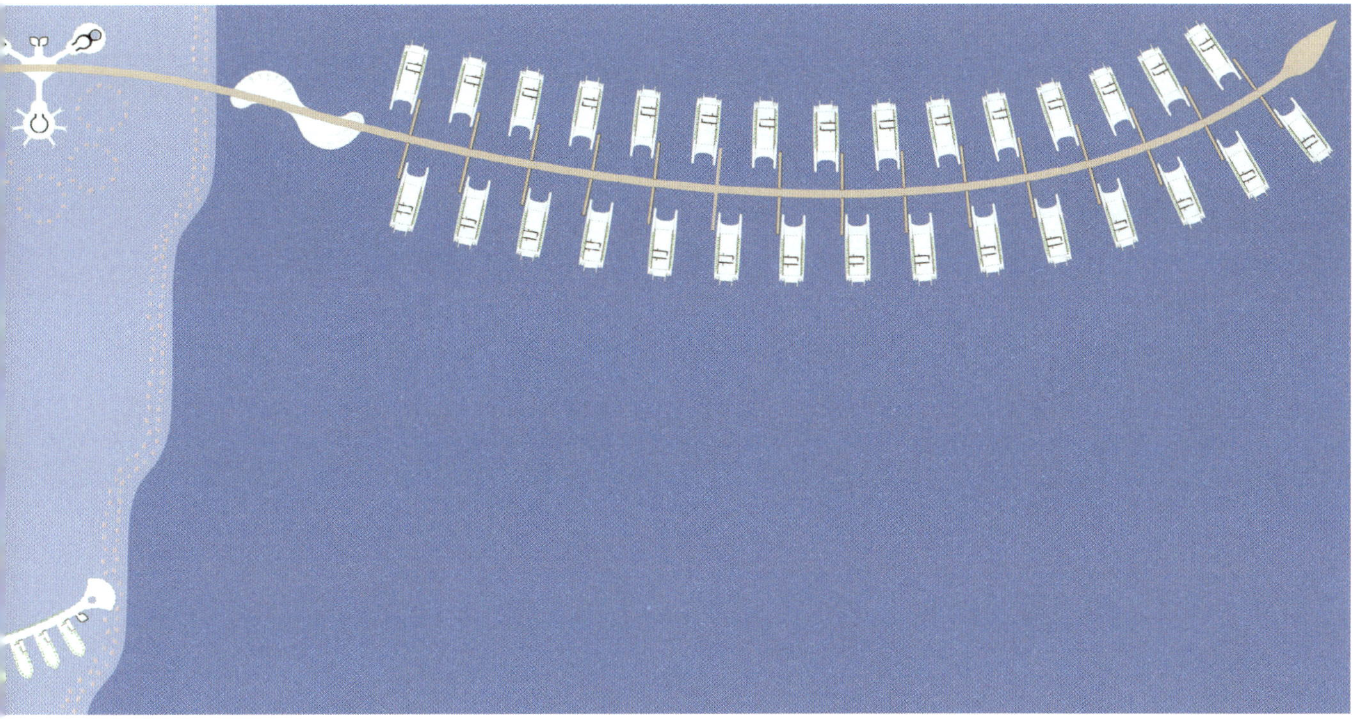

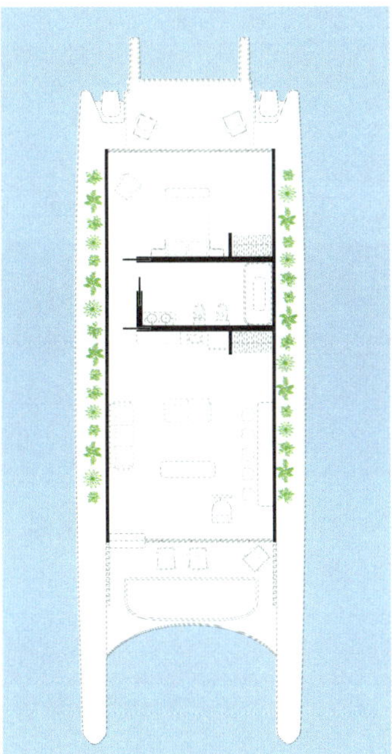

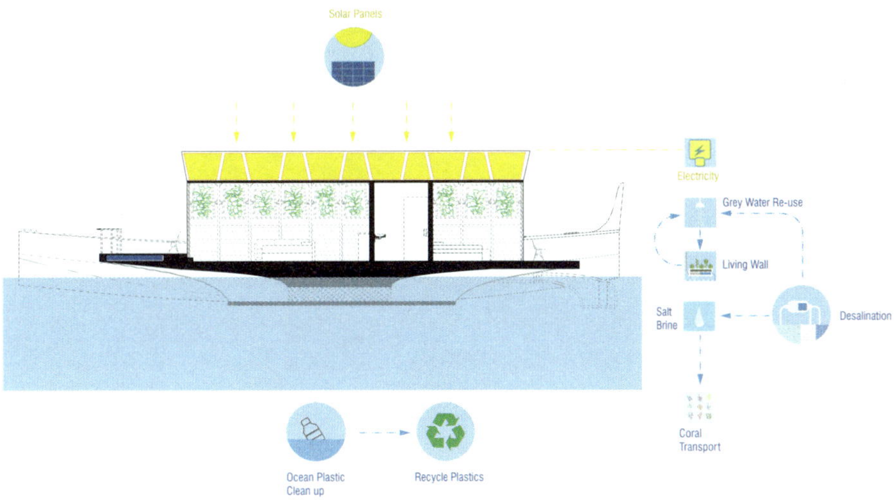
Solar Panels
Electricity
Grey Water Re-use
Living Wall
Salt
Brine
Desalination
Coral
Transport
Ocean Plastic
Clean up
Recycle Plastics

ABOVE: View from beach toward floating spa and Gili Trawangan

Laélia Kim-Lan Vaulot
Natural History

Indonesia lies within the Coral Triangle of biodiversity. Coastal populations once relied on a bounteous sea for food and economic activity. Over the last 15 years the fish population has declined drastically due to the increase in human population and market expansion. Currently the interests of tourists visiting the Gili Islands and the local community are misaligned. Tourists come to observe marine life, while the local population still relies on fishing to survive.

Seaweed farming has been encouraged by environmental agencies as a restorative alternative economy. Hydrocolloids, the gels contained in seaweed used in many industries, are in high demand. Currently 80 percent of the seaweed farmed in Indonesia is processed in the Philippines. Farmers fail to capture an important part of the economic value as the raw material goes through layers of treatment and trade. The Natural History resort supports the local economy with a processing facility to extract hydrocolloids from seaweed produced by farms around the island. Community members farm and process the seaweed on the resort site to generate sustainable revenues.

The resort also champions eco-responsible tourism with a focus on marine exploration through scuba diving, biology courses, and underwater photography to survey and raise awareness of the underwater ecosystems. Tourists experience the beneficial properties of seaweed through spa treatments and traditional Indonesian seaweed salad, made with local bananas, chilies, and sugarcane. They can also buy locally made products derived from seaweed.

This project is inspired by the ocean ecosystem, particularly how marine species have smart ways of cohabiting in symbiotic relationships, often between animal and vegetal organisms. In turn, the resort fosters a symbiotic relationship between its own program and structure, tourists, and local residents.

ABOVE: Front of House. From the dive center a cart, pulled by one of the hotel's three local ponies, leads customers to the reception.

OPPOSITE: Bar, Gallery and Library. The building on the right hosts the bar, a gallery where underwater photographs and drawings can be exhibited, and a library.

View from beach toward the floating spa and Gili Trawangan

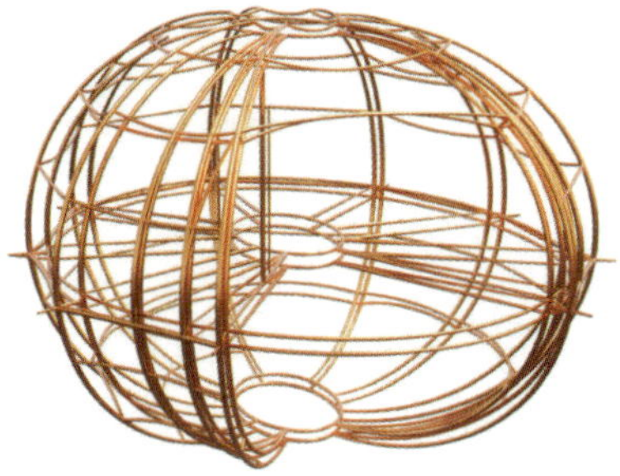

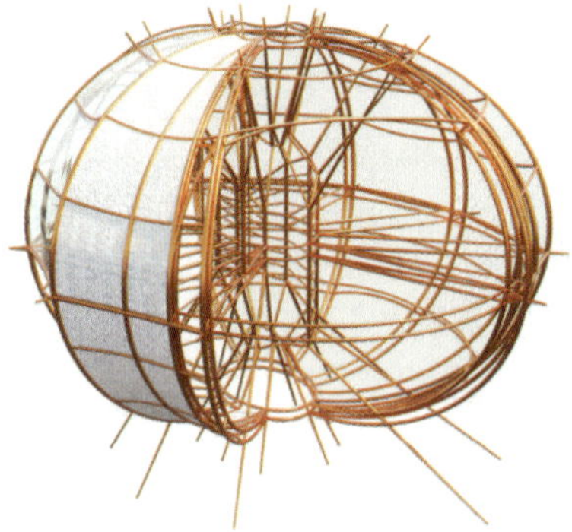

LEFT: Villa at 7 a.m., 1 p.m., and 6 p.m. The villa allows a full experience of the sea through its translucent skin.

RIGHT: Villas are constructed using prefabricated metal ribs forming the quarters of the volumes.

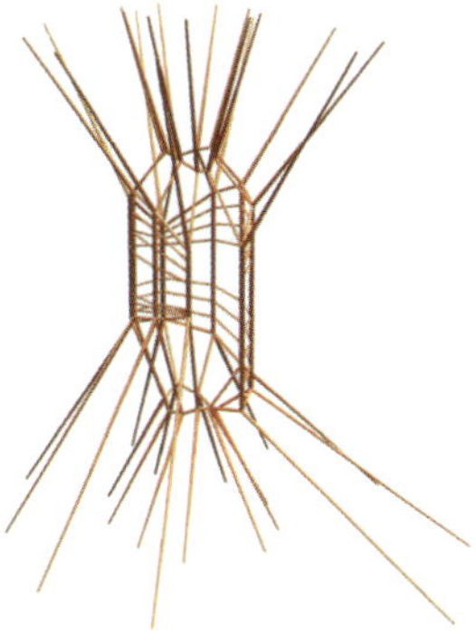

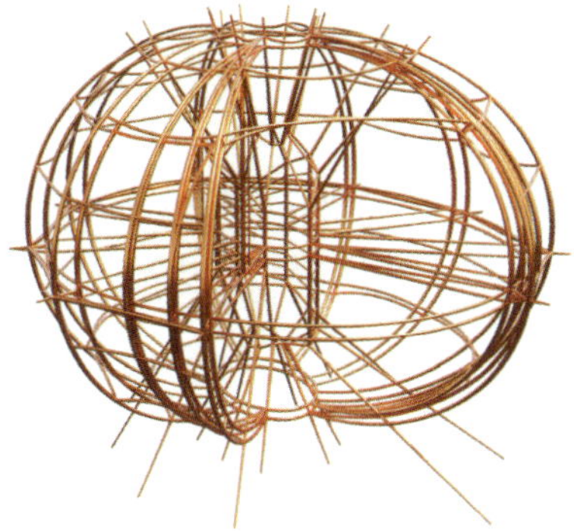

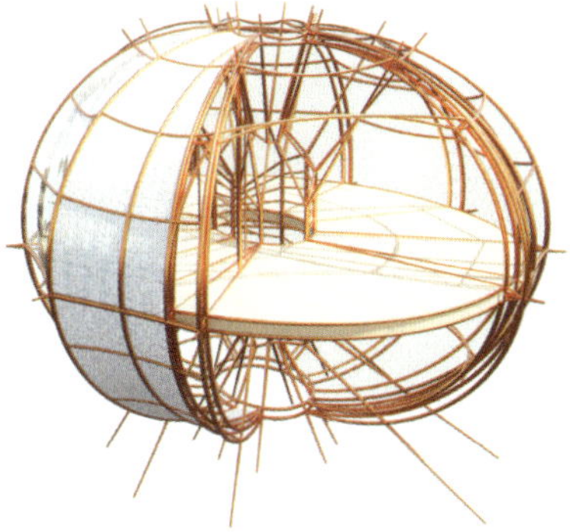

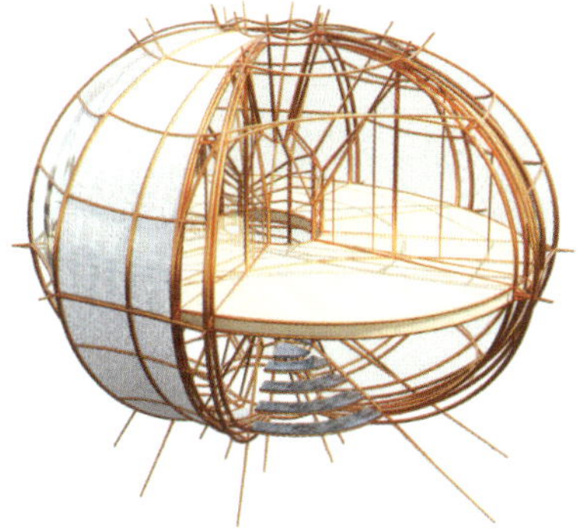

ZONES

SKY

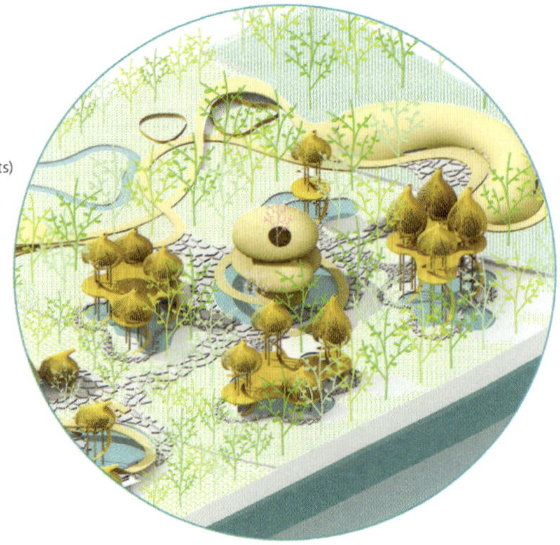

LAGOON

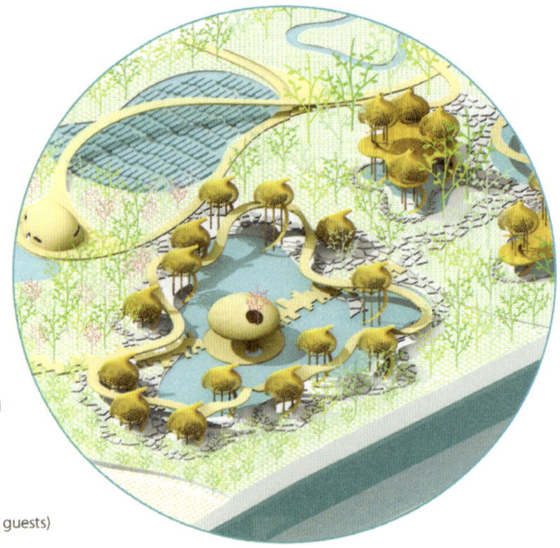

UNDER THE SEA AND BEACH

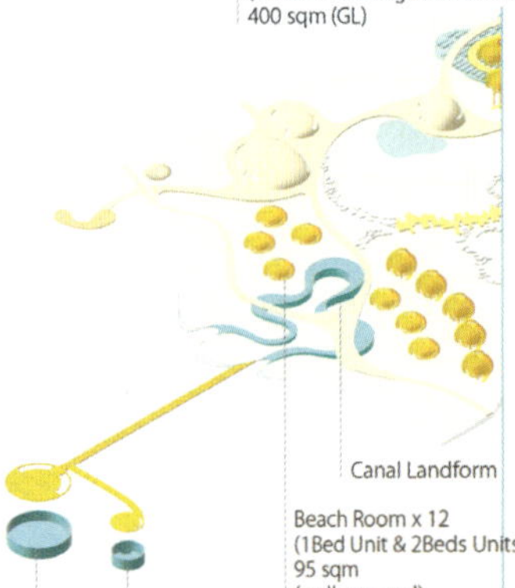

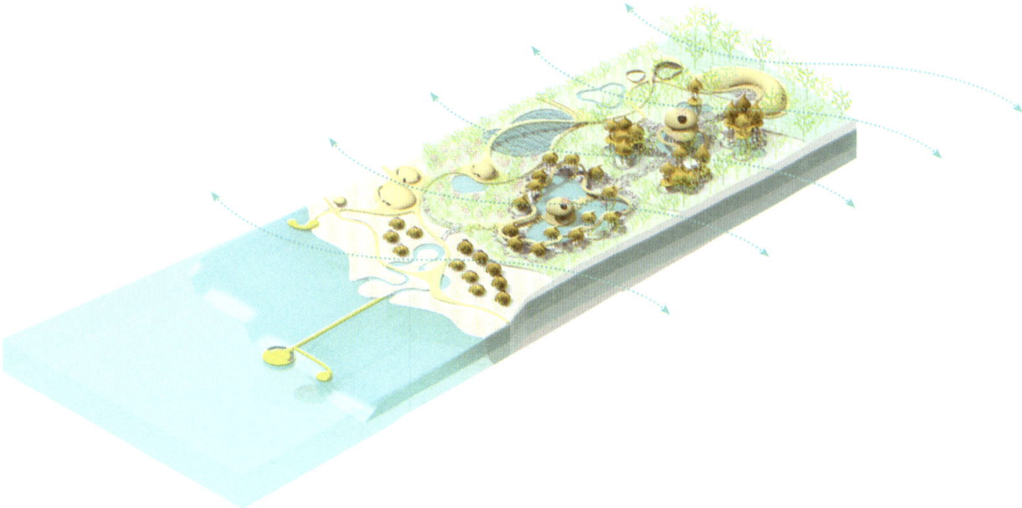

I-Ting Tsai
Selalu Cinta

Selalu Cinta responds to the unique geology and biology of Gili Meno while targeting the destination wedding industry in Indonesia. The resort provides a unique sustainable experience centered on wedding couples, their families and friends, and honeymooners with on-site wedding venues, blocks of bedrooms for large parties, and romantic amenities. The self-sustaining resort includes farms and ranches. Local plants enhance biodiversity and walkway shading; ocean breezes flow through building apertures. The resort complex can harvest rainwater, reclaim wastewater, activate a seawater cooling system, and generate power with solar shingle roofs. With this design the development will give back more to the environment than it takes away.

Various organizational zones—Under the Sea, Beach, Lagoon, and Sky—provide guests with different spatial experiences. Indigenous architectural forms, materials, and building techniques create new double-skin bamboo facades that blend into the local cultural context. Bamboo wraps from a bulbous shape up around a stone base to an angled point to facilitate the flow of air and heat. The buildings are prefabricated at different scales based on the program and assembled on-site, minimizing the impact of the construction process on the natural environment.

Using environmental data and simulating the tropical climate through computational fluid dynamics (CFD), the design was optimized for natural cooling, enhancing airflow with stack ventilation in each room. Selalu Cinta operates with a reduced ecological footprint and carbon emissions to provide guests with a sustainable resort lifestyle.

ABOVE: Axon showing room orientation and doors in relation to natural ventilation of ocean breeze

OPPOSITE: Axon diagrams of Under the Sea, Beach, Lagoon, and Sky zones

View toward Selalu Cinta on the beaches of Gili Meno

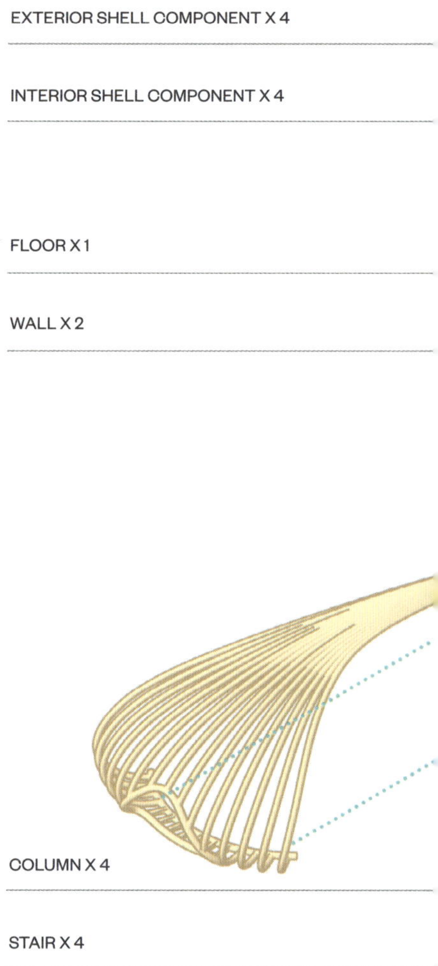

ABOVE TOP: The villa skin is made of dead coral aggregate, allowing light through and transforming the structure into a nocturnal lantern floating on the water.

ABOVE BOTTOM: Development of the structure through the study of natural heating and cooling systems

RIGHT: Prefabrication assembly sequence for bamboo modules

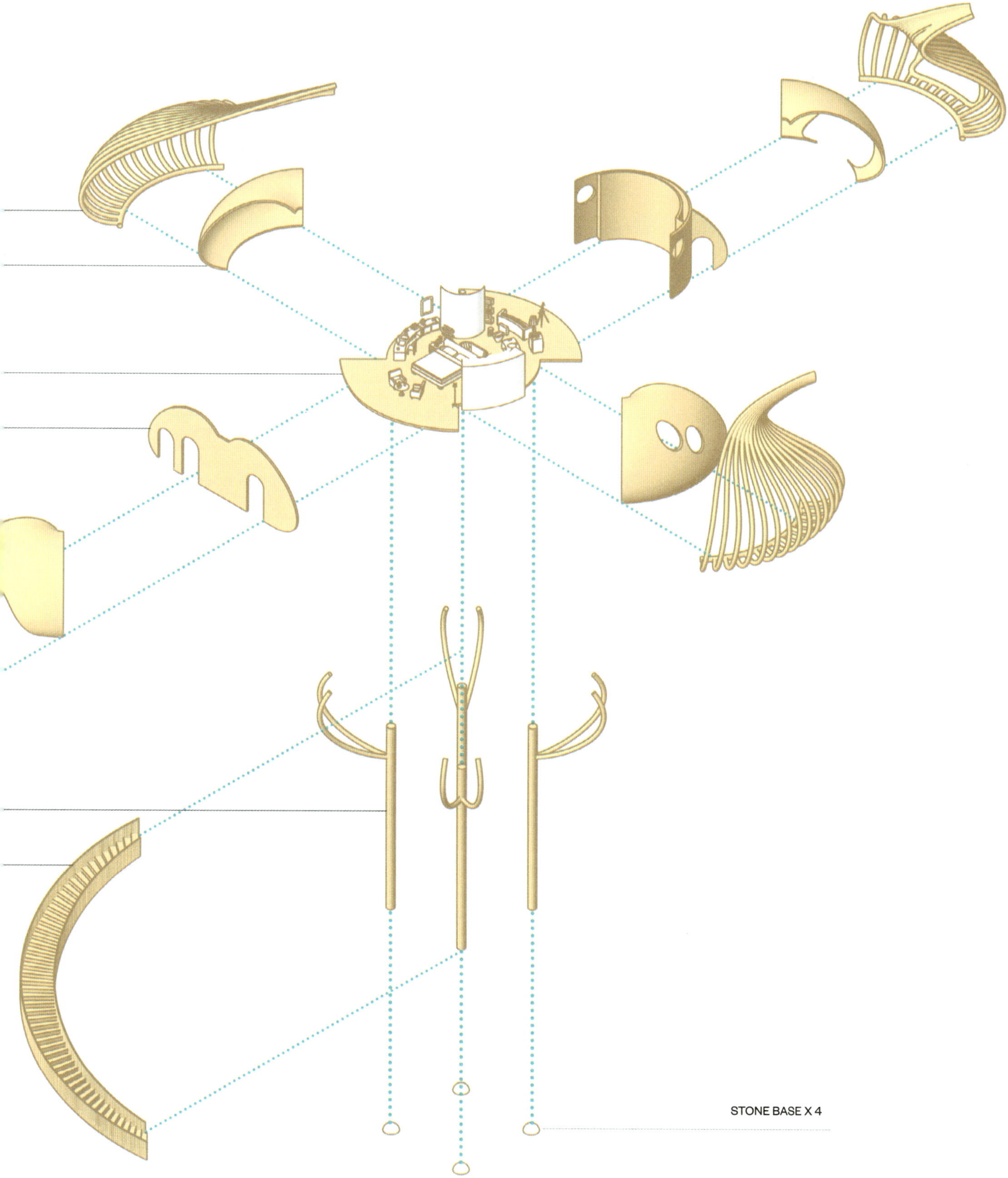
STONE BASE X 4

Cristina Anastase
The Conservatory

The Conservatory is a resort that minimizes environmental impact and turns tourism into an opportunity to regenerate the existing ecosystem. Sited in a coral and botanical garden, the resort addresses the multiple issues that arise when developing on tropical islands such as Gili Meno.

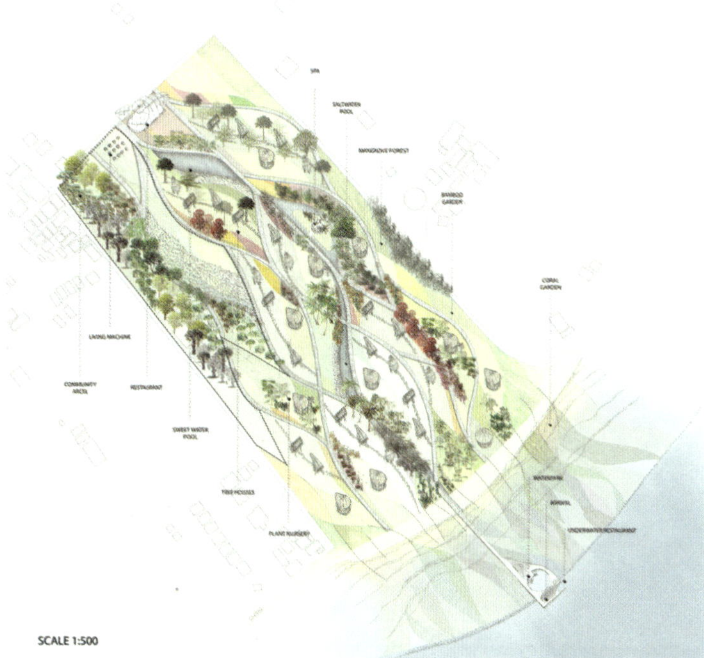

Requiring significant offshore resources, typical resorts on small islands are detrimental to the natural environment in the quest to create memorable tourist experiences. At the Conservatory native flora and fauna species are regenerated in botanical gardens. Local bamboo, palms, and coconut and banana trees supply food and construction materials so that Gili Meno is less dependent on external resources. A new coral garden is an extension of ongoing coral-reef regeneration initiatives.

Staying at the Conservatory offers a very different experience from that of a typical resort; it is more than just temporary accommodation. Guests participate in shaping and nurturing the landscape by planting native species in the botanical and underwater coral gardens while building a relationship with the spaces. They can meander through a network of garden paths, experience living in a tree house, or explore the coral reef in a symbiotic relationship with the natural environment.

ABOVE: Master plan

OPPOSITE: One-bedroom units and botanical garden

Underwater coral reef Bar

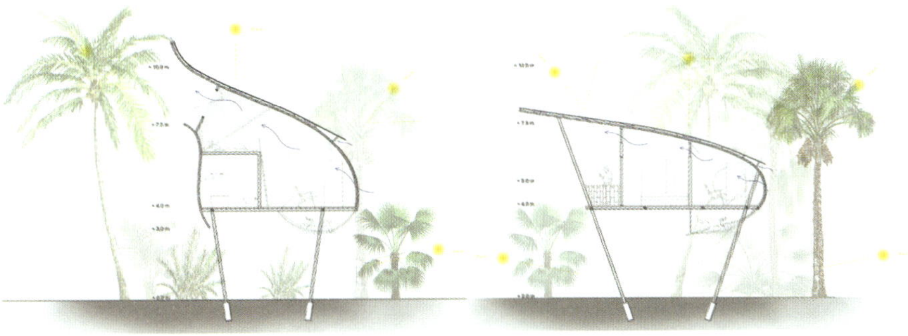

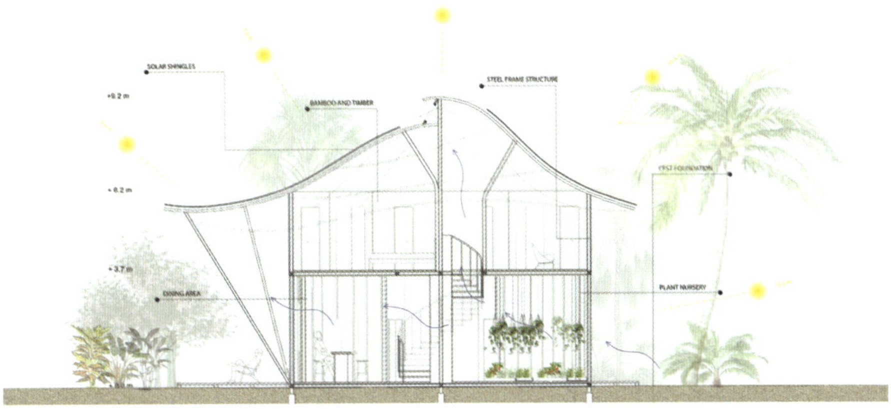

LEFT: Arrival area, water park, and underwater restaurant

TOP: One-bedroom units, section

BOTTOM: Two-bedroom unit, section

HEALTH RESORTS

Health Resorts focus on the mental and physical wellness of guests through programs such as spas, dance and music venues, meditation pavilions, and much more. These projects frame Gili Meno as an island retreat away from the fast-paced modern world that enhances guests' health and well-being through relaxing activities and local crafts.

OPPOSITE: Elaine Cui, interior of restaurant looking toward beach bar

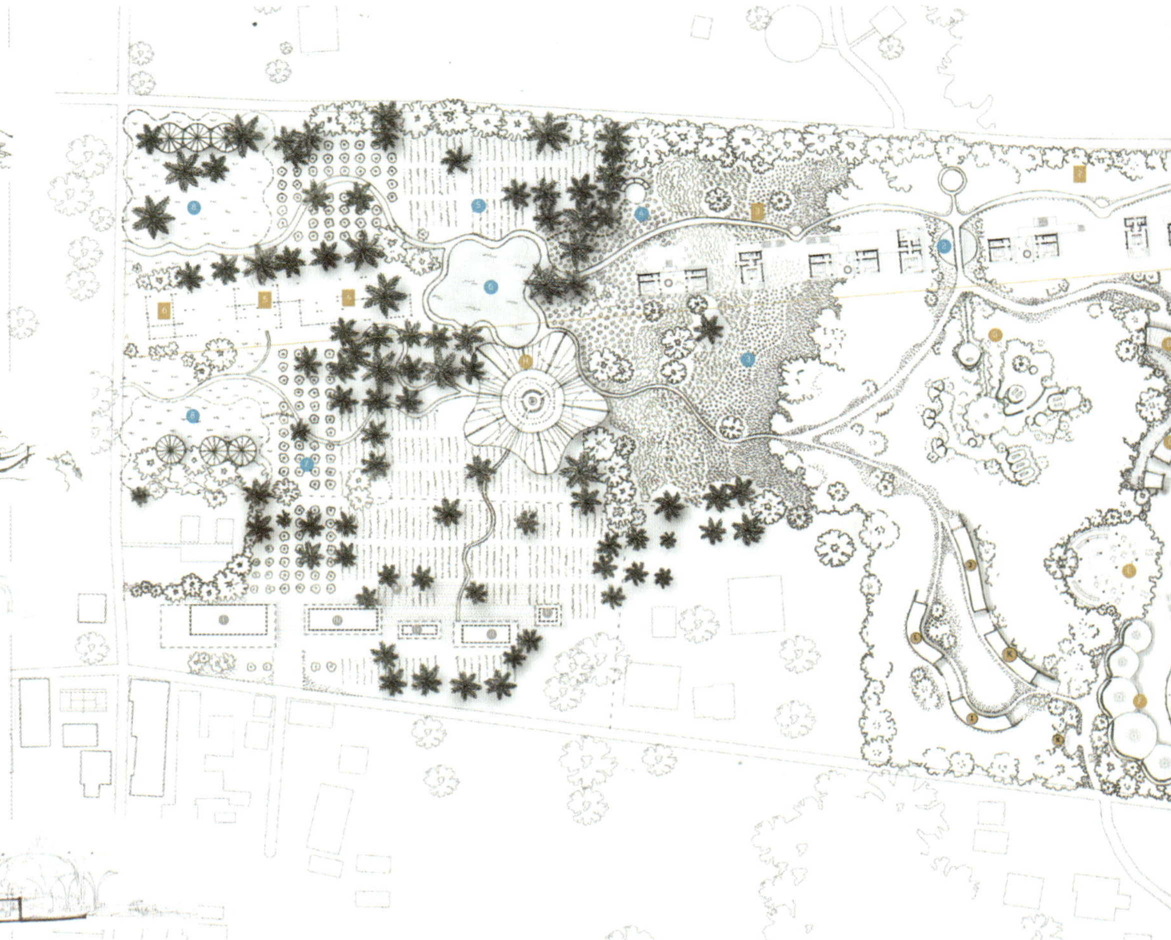

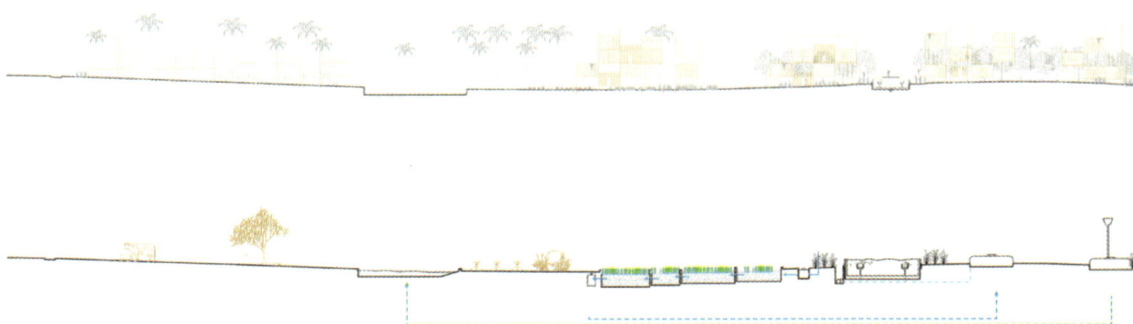

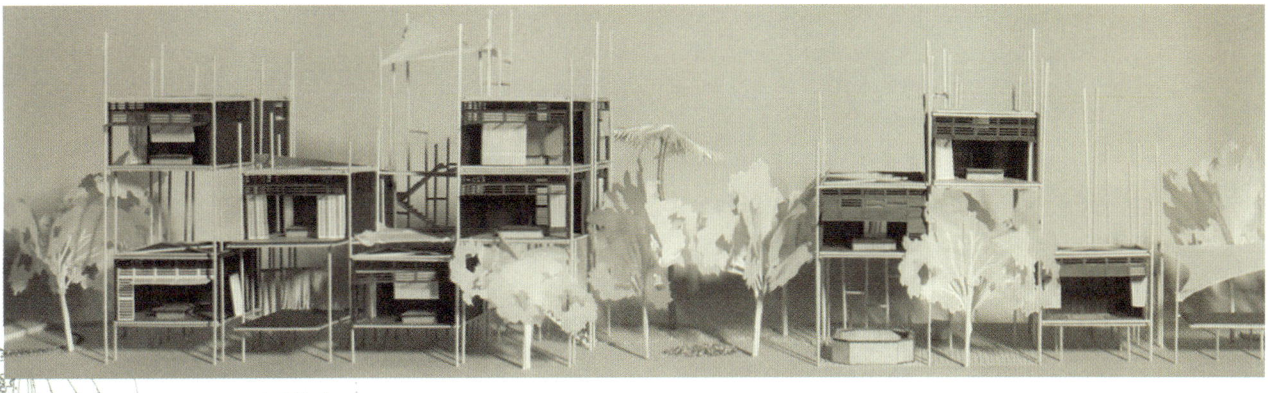

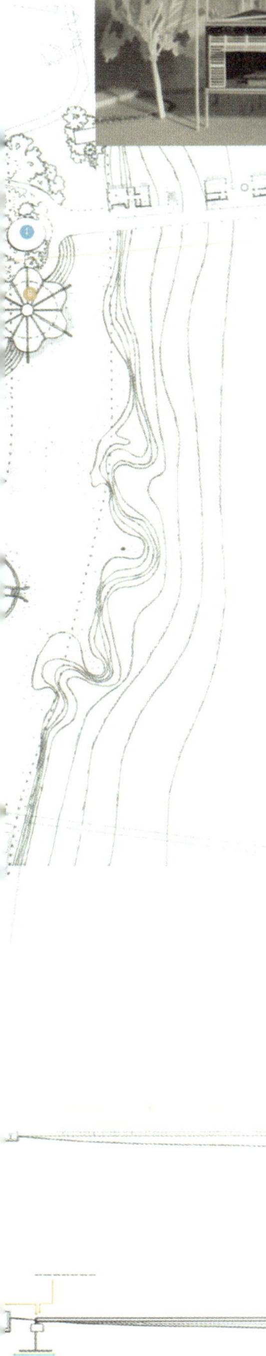

Samantha Monge Kaser
Alam

Alam embraces the remote island as a comprehensive vacation experience for its guests. Through a carefully tailored community lifestyle and programming sequence, the resort allows guests to slow down and recharge body and soul. This coliving structure sets a vibrant yet soothing tone through a combination of ultimate comfort and carefully crafted programming, promising an integrated retreat from twenty-first-century stress.

Alam creates a variety of experiences that comprise the rhythm of daily life. These include daily rituals such as morning fishing outings and the making of flower offerings by folding palm-leaf baskets for the local Hindu deities, as well as seasonal programming grouped into categories like nature and science, arts and crafts, health and wellness, and music and dance. Bookings have minimum length requirements depending on a specific program's duration. Resident experts are core to the experience and, along with the staff and guests, add to the richness of the Alam family.

Through its carefully crafted programming and amenities, Alam emphasizes interpersonal exchanges and keeps private space to the essentials, expanding opportunities for socialization and time outdoors. Guests can enjoy the social zone at the beachside restaurants and lounge or a central Zen zone with space for health and wellness activities. A block of housing units to the north is organized in a regular grid of bamboo and recycled timber, while its vast amenity spaces follow organic curves made of unbaked clay bricks that interweave with the landscaped grounds. From its local construction materials and passive modular design to its programmed booking packages, Alam provides a holistic and sustainable approach to tourism.

LEFT: Master plan and section strategy of Zen and social zones

ABOVE: Model elevation

Axonometric of beachfront amenities

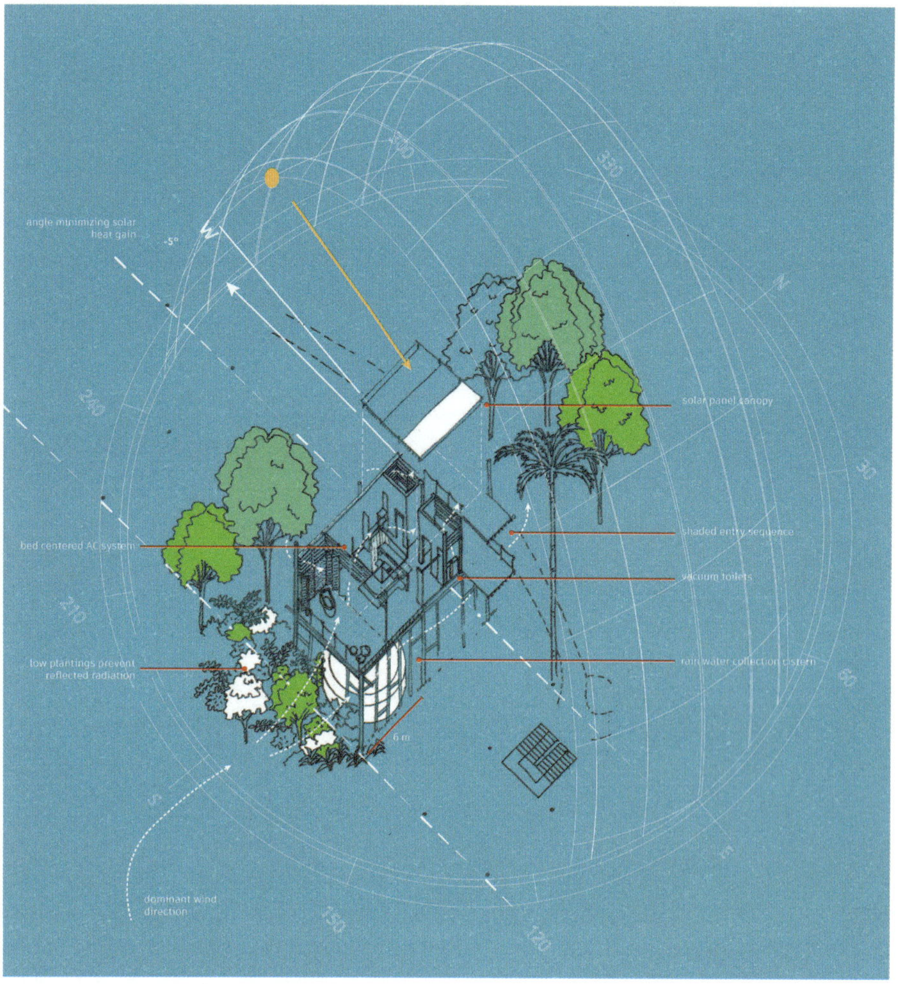

ABOVE: Environmental axon of prototypical unit

OPPOSITE: Model detail

Jenna Ritz
Cahaya

Located on a remote island with limited resources and high seismic activity, Cahaya is intimately connected to its ecologically diverse site. The design and program of this wellness retreat responds to Gili Meno's three distinct environments: Sea, Land, and Sky. The built interventions are tailored to each zone and generate varied atmospheres to cultivate a deep connection between guests and the surrounding landscape. The opportunity to interact intimately with various natural habitats inspires a range of tailored retreat experiences enhanced by the architectural design.

The Sea Village floats over the water off the coast, opening outward for views of the vast expanse of the ocean and the morning sunrise over the adjacent island. The Jungle Spa is nestled in the lush landscape at the heart of the retreat, emphasizing its importance to rejuvenating the body as part of the wellness journey. The multiple spa buildings are connected through a series of paths and views dictated by existing foliage and strategic building placement to create an active sanctuary for introspection.

The Sky Villas are elevated to the height of the local palm trees to maximize views across the entire island while serving as a safe haven for tsunami refuge. Though separated into three distinct zones, each village is housed in structures with bamboo construction to establish material continuity through the resort. The flexible nature of the bamboo provides a resilient measure against future earthquakes and tsunamis. Cahaya cultivates a transformative wellness journey by developing a strong sense of place through the integration of nature and use of local materials.

ABOVE: Cross-section of Sky Villa with walkway

OPPOSITE: Longitudinal section of Sky Villa among the palm trees

View toward spa reception building among the foliage

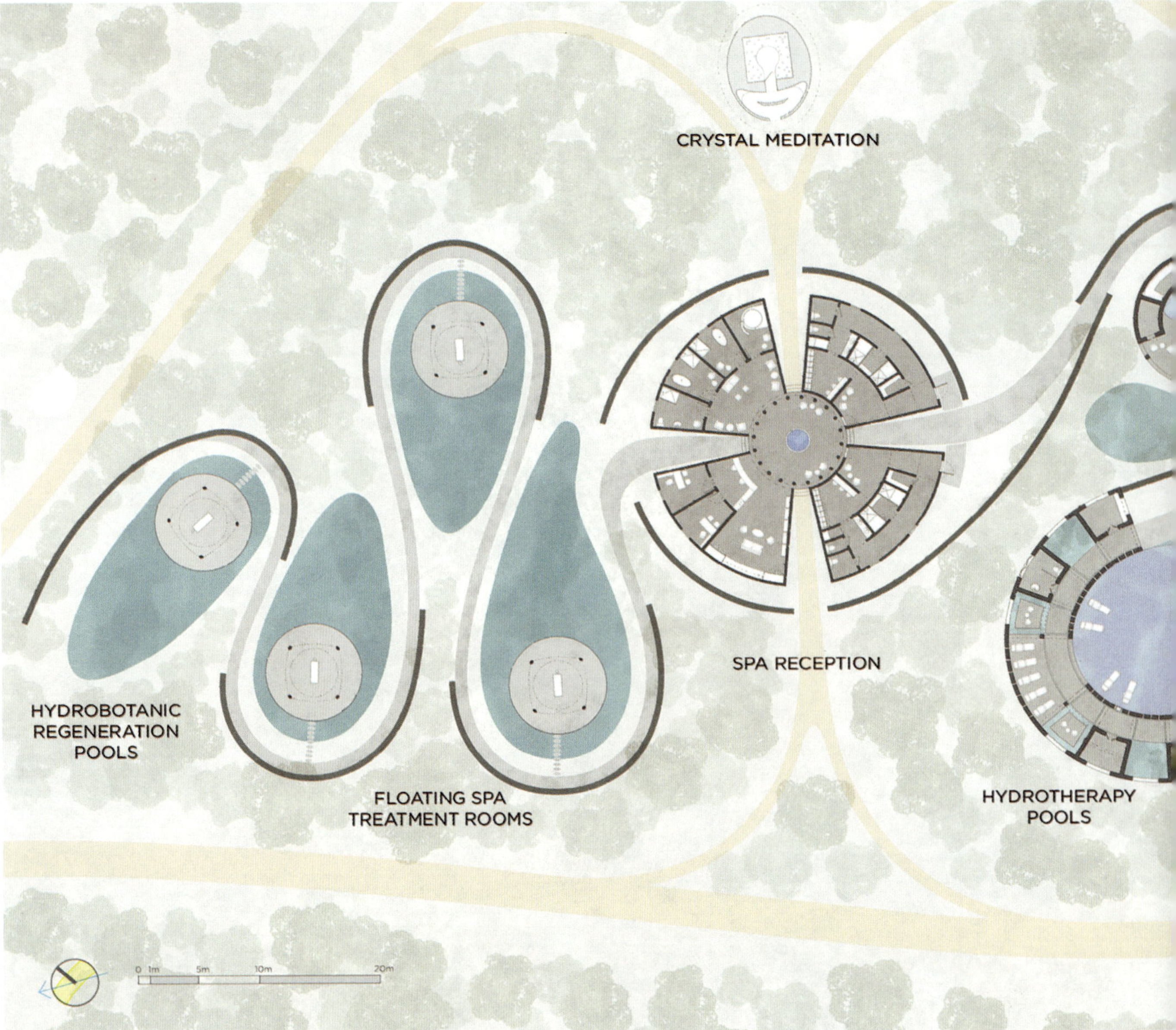
CRYSTAL MEDITATION
HYDROBOTANIC
REGENERATION
POOLS
FLOATING SPA
TREATMENT ROOMS
SPA RECEPTION
HYDROTHERAPY
POOLS
0 1m 5m 10m 20m

LEFT: Floor plan of the Jungle Spa surrounded by hydrobotanic pools

TOP RIGHT: Master plan of Cahaya wellness retreat on Gili Meno

BOTTOM RIGHT: Section through floating spa treatment rooms and hydrobotanic regeneration pools

Elaine Cui
Sehat

Sehat is a mental-health retreat that provides time, space, and support to focus on healing. One in four people in the world are affected by mental or neurological disorders at some point in their lives. Around 450 million people currently suffer from such conditions, placing mental disorders among the leading causes of ill health and disability worldwide.

Indonesia lies within the Coral Triangle of biodiversity, and Sehat is a tropical sanctuary providing guests an opportunity to take a break from daily life and focus on wellness. The resort hosts 33 units for a total of 40 to 70 guests. Inspired by the nervous system, the design divides hotel programs into three zones connected by bamboo-covered walkways: time and space, support and therapy, healing and rejuvenation. Visitors enter from the oceanfront and are greeted by the reception, a restaurant, and a bar. After arriving at hotel units, guests travel through a series of private therapeutic pavilions in the middle of the site. After the long hike from the pavilions, visitors terminate the healing journey at the meditation pavilion, which symbolizes a sense of rejuvenation.

The resort's passive environmental design strategy features a water-treatment journey. Seawater at the front of the site will be treated throughout by aquaponics along with gray-water recycling and rainwater irrigation. A new waste center incorporating the micro-auto gasification system is designed on adjacent community land. The meditation pavilion has a 150-person occupancy and can be used as a shelter in case of natural disasters.

ABOVE: Interior view of spa pavilion

OPPOSITE: Plan of beach restaurant and bar with walkways

ABOVE: Interior view of a service in meditation pavilion

OPPOSITE: Diagram and Sections of the impact of solar and water interventions on site

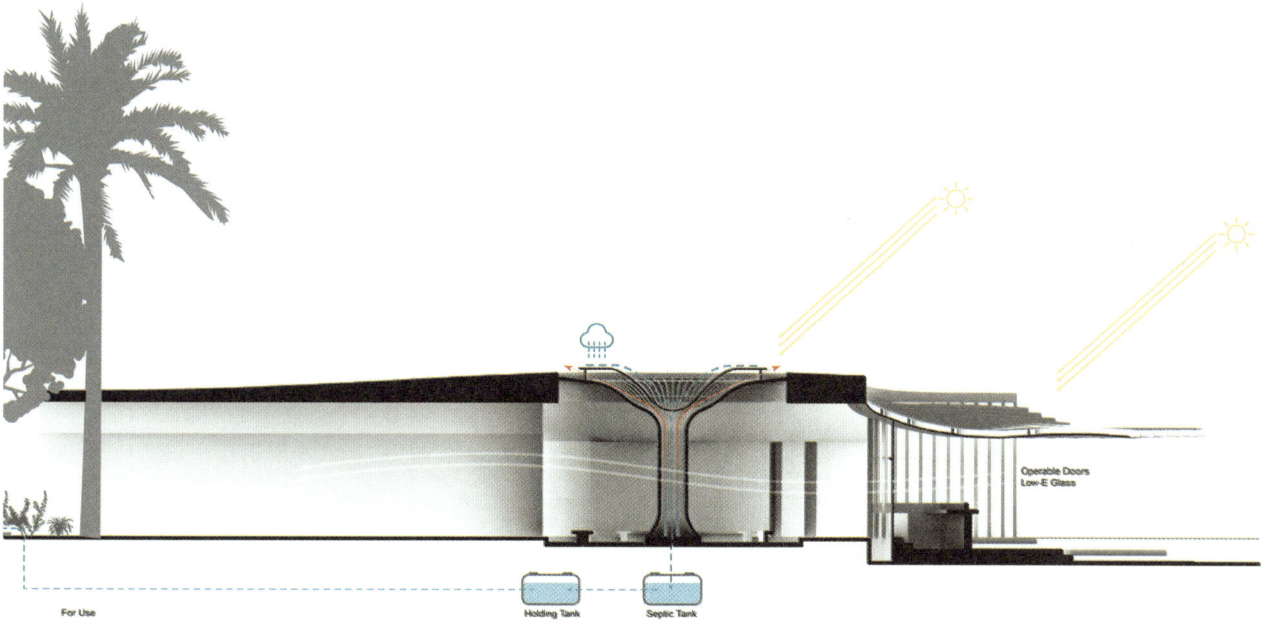
Operable Doors
Low-E Glass
For Use
Holding Tank
Septic Tank

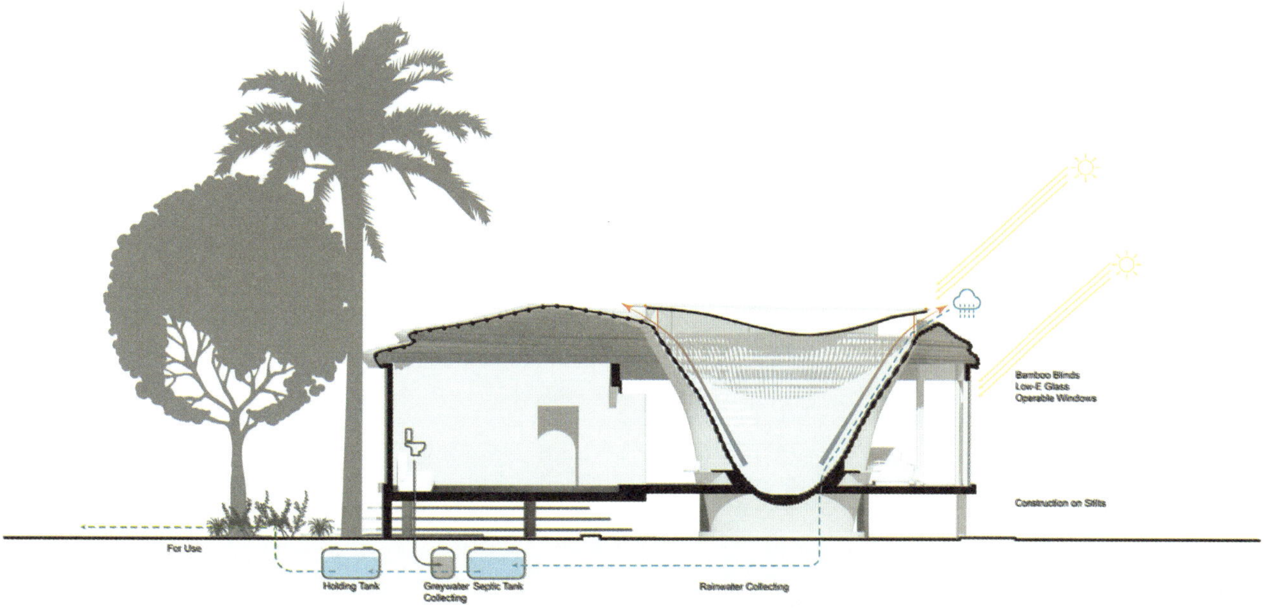
Bamboo Blinds
Low-E Glass
Operable Windows
Construction on Stilts
For Use
Holding Tank
Greywater Collecting
Septic Tank
Rainwater Collecting

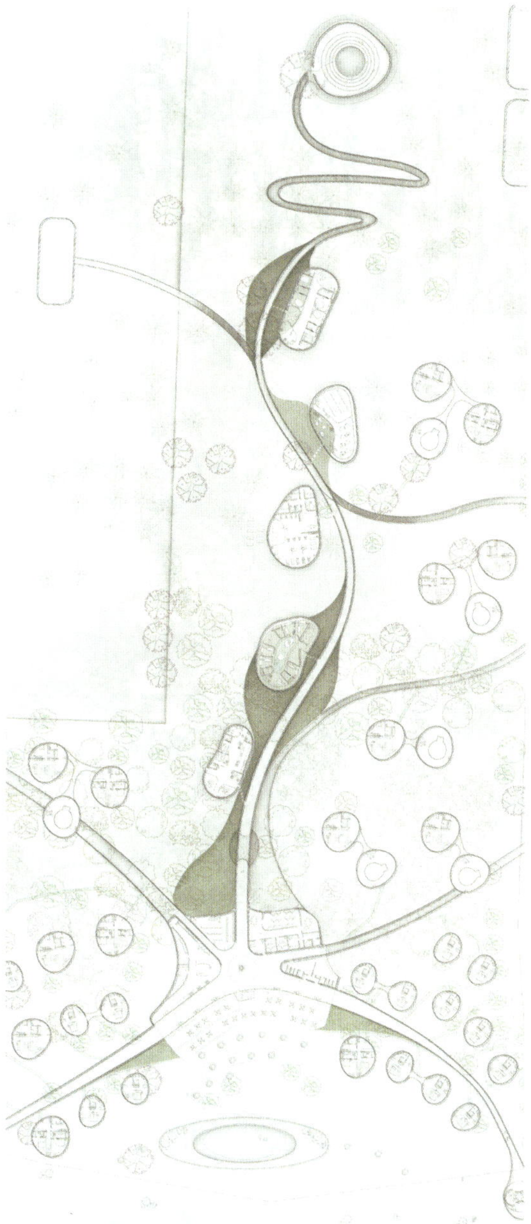

LEFT: Master plan showing the three zones: time and space, support and therapy, healing and rejuvenation

RIGHT: View of reception center on the beach

CONVERSATION WITH JOHN SPENCE: INDUSTRY RESPONSE TO ECO-RESORTS

Many student projects proposed new models of tourism, and in light of the COVID-19 crisis many companies have explored new ways to connect and adapt to the changing times. Karma Resorts has launched Karma Community. What opportunities do you see in exploring alternative forms of tourism in the future as a result of the studio and the difficulties this year?

JOHN SPENCE: The current situation has certainly made us rethink and look at different tourism models. It is very much a time of domestic tourism. Clearly our previous model was predicated on people holidaying internationally in exotic locations. That is just not possible now because either our locations aren't open to certain people coming in or certain people can't leave their countries for various destinations. But it doesn't mean that people don't want to go on holiday. When our resorts are open we have seen stellar success. Over the last few months our resorts in England have been populated by English guests, our resorts in India by Indians, and so on.

Taking that further, we are developing self-contained RVs that people can drive to our Karma destinations or campsites so they can be outside or in a "bubble" with their family or friends. We started by working with existing camper firms. Our plan is to make our own bespoke camper vans that can operate off-grid to have their own power, water, and sewerage. We're looking at working with a company that makes vans and buses for touring bands to create our own travel units as a mobile Karma Resort. People could spend one or two days at one resort and then move to another. We see an opportunity for standalone leasable vans with sleeping berths. Other vans or larger buses could have social components that travel to different destinations. After being in a bubble, one could be tested for COVID-19 before getting on the bus to travel and take in the scenery.

The other concept we're looking at is called Karma Casa as a response to domestic tourism. We are considering acquiring resorts that are within one or two hours of major metropolitan areas where we have large memberships. Rather than people going to our resorts for their annual holidays, they could go to Karma Casa daily or weekly. There they can set up their laptops, connect to dedicated hotspot desks, and host meetings with clients or colleagues. They can have business lunches and enjoy the sports facilities while their children enjoy the

OPPOSITE: Karma Reef, Beachfront Bungalow, Gili Meno

kids club. Then maybe in the evening they have a fantastic dinner with their partner.

What was the inception of the Karma Community model and how has it been received so far?

COVID-19 has forced us to be extremely close to our members and clients. So we focused on creating interaction and opening our communication channels through Karma Community. I personally speak to my owners once a week, and we have town halls in an attempt to go the extra mile. With global uncertainty people need communication. They need to understand that they're a part of a club that is listening and talking to them. I think that everyone understands there will be challenges and problems. But Karma Community has been vital: the loyalty of our owners has been extremely encouraging, and we've seen fantastic traction and bookings.

In 28 years of operation have there been other moments of significant change that have helped to spur on what are now seen as standard industry practices, and what were they?

There's nothing as certain as change. We've been through epidemics, earthquakes, tsunamis, volcanic eruptions, famines, a currency crisis, and the current pandemic. You have to respond and react. I always quote John Madden, who coached the Dallas Cowboys, and Alex Ferguson, former manager of Manchester United: "The secret to success is not spending time worrying about where you can't effect change, but spending time worrying about where you can."

Over the last few years Asia has emerged as a source of tourists. When we started there were primarily European and American visitors, and now we see more Indian, Chinese, and Southeast Asian guests at our resorts. We've also seen a huge rise in awareness of sustainability in terms of holidaying patterns and resort developments. I wouldn't say that 30 years ago people were blind to these issues, but there's certainly much more education

and consciousness now about global warming and other issues. So whether a developer sincerely believes that they need to incorporate sustainability or sees a commercial advantage in being sustainable, there's no discrepancy. A commercial advantage actually validates the need to be sustainable because there's nothing less sustainable than a failed resort. So more developers and hoteliers are embracing sustainability. Educated consumers with more awareness of natural disasters see that the earth is fragile and tend to support hoteliers who have the same mindset. We

have clients from Southeast Asia, India, and Sri Lanka who are concerned about the environment and make sure that the resorts are conscious of it as well.

The current pandemic has led to a radical shift in how companies work internally through adopting tech for web-based meetings and exploring new support models for workers at resorts. What changes do you see as being temporary, and what do you see as a potential new permanent model for Karma?

We have a love-hate relationship with Zoom. There's no question whatsoever that Zoom has been hugely beneficial. We have totally adapted and pivoted how we communicate with each other. For example, my managing director is locked down in Brisbane, my sales and marketing director is in New South Wales, my chief operations officer is in Bali, and my regional sales director is in India, and we have not met each other since March apart from online.

If we had this pandemic more than ten or more years ago, who knows how much harder it would be to do business and get on with life. So clearly it's been fantastic. My concern with online work is that it does not replace human interaction. We were negotiating a deal in Germany online, and we encountered a lot of pushback and friction. There were various stakeholders, lawyers, and accountants, among others. It wasn't a deal breaker, but certainly it wasn't going as smooth as either party wanted. The day the quarantine measures were lifted I got on a plane and went to Germany. In one day I met with the key stakeholders and ended up having lunch with the lawyer and the principal

ABOVE: Karma Kandara, the Luxury Grand Cliff-Front Residence, Bali

OPPOSITE: Karma Kandara, Villa Interior, Bali

people on the other side. Every single problem was washed away over the course of a few hours with a good bottle of wine, something to eat, conversations about our families, and a couple of jokes. One of the dangers of online meetings is that companies have become very reliant on it. It's important to have a balance. Going forward we will certainly use technology more—there is a cost-saving aspect for meetings—but I'll be very careful to keep that human interaction. As humans we like to meet, bond, and do things personally.

You plan to focus on building sustainable designs for Karma Sanctum Bali and Karma Bequia, however Karma has also acquired older properties. Do you find these older structures to be as sustainable and efficient as they were when they were designed, before the current ideas concerning HVAC?

We do one of two things: we take a piece of land and develop it or we buy or lease an existing property and renovate it, but there is a trade-off. At Caux-et-Sauzens, in France, there is a 600–700 square-meter château and farmhouse with really thick stone walls. As a heritage building it reflects southern France, and the building preservation codes prevent us from stashing HVAC on the roof. It's a balance: you can't always build a pure sustainable building with an aesthetic that's necessarily going to be in tune with the local environment. You've got to make an effort to combine sustainability with the existing fabric. That's one of the nice challenges; otherwise it would be boring. I like the opportunity of having a clean slate and a bit of land, but it's also fantastic to take something that's already there and remodel it attractively so you can have a nod to both sustainability and the past.

What do you view as one of the most misunderstood aspects of sustainability at a resort?

First a resort has to be sustainable as a viable commercial proposition for many years. That is absolutely key. There's nothing worse on the planet than a resort that goes bankrupt because a developer was too focused on sustainability and has more money going out than coming in. Are consumers savvy toward sustainability? Yes, of course. Is it the be-all and end-all? No.

Karma Kandara, Beach Club, Bali

People want to relax and enjoy themselves on holiday. So if a resort has won an award for sustainability but is dull and sterile or not attractive, people will not go there. They might praise it in articles, but a resort is a commercial proposition, and someone has to pay you suitable money to stay there to cover the costs of development and operation with enough margin for profit.

Supply chains and local infrastructure are some of the most critical aspects to maintain the flow of energy and food to a resort, as well as build connections with the local community. Does a more sustainable and self-sufficient resort present new challenges in building those community relationships?

A resort such as Karma Kandara, in Bali, is part of a greater community. Most of our employees are from the Banjar villages. It's a back-scratching relationship. We are delighted and honor-bound to support the local community with jobs. Now we are providing more than 800 people with monthly food packages due to unemployment, and we support the local football team. We are dependent on each other and need to work closely together. Often multinational companies fail in Indonesia, Sri Lanka, and India because they don't understand the importance of community relations. You have to be part of the local community because it can dictate what happens more than the official central government. Karma Borgo di Colleoli sits in a little hamlet in Tuscany where we have a church and we rely on the community. Karma St. Martin's, on the Isles of Scilly, employs half of the 140 local residents through the hotel, restaurant, and bar. Even if the local community embraces sustainable practices at resorts, I don't think it makes a huge difference to these relationships. You can't always be sustainable in terms of food, for example: you might grow or produce some of the food, but you still rely on the local community in the process.

You mentioned that since the prohibition on air travel began you saw a noticeable improvement in the atmosphere due to the lack of pollution, and during the studio several students explored eco-friendly methods of tourist travel. How do you view the future of travel and transportation in light of COVID-19?

Over the last few months I have been privileged to be able to travel to the Greek islands, Florence, and Rome, and I didn't see any major pollution due to the lack of tourist traffic in the form of airplanes and cars. I have a house in England, near Heathrow, and usually the sky is crisscrossed with planes. Now every day during lockdown I walk the dogs on the Ascot racecourse, and I've never seen the sky bluer, clearer, or cleaner. Going forward I think there is going to be a balance. I don't believe that people are going to stop flying. Business travel may decrease a bit due to the cost savings associated with online meetings. One of the biggest concerns is actually the economic fallout over the next few years due to the pandemic. I think we're going to see a recession that will affect airlines. Once there is a big pickup in flights again it will be the Chinese and Indian tourists who will want to see the world and travel first. As long as the pandemic affects flight restrictions, concerns about health and safety, and financial concerns, tourist travel is going to suffer, and there'll be a lot less travel in the next few years. But when people can travel again, they certainly will.

Wishing you all the best from Gili Meno!

Image Credits

Antonio Citterio Patricia Viel and Partners / Rio Helmi: 39-41; DUS Architects / Ossip van Duivenbode and Sophia van den Hoek: 44, 45; Karma Group: 26, 27, 128, 130-132, 134, 135; Squire and Partners: 14-21; Fery Kurniawan / IPB University: 30, 32, 33; IBUKU: 48, 50-52, 54, 55; SAOTA / Adam Letch: 42, 43; Rukshan Vathupola: 31, 32, 47,49; WOHA architects / Patrick Bingham-Hall: 36-38